Artificial Intelligence
for Computer Games

Artificial Intelligence for Computer Games

An Introduction

John David Funge

CRC Press
Taylor & Francis Group
Boca Raton London New York

CRC Press is an imprint of the
Taylor & Francis Group, an **informa** business

AN A K PETERS BOOK

CRC Press
Taylor & Francis Group
6000 Broken Sound Parkway NW, Suite 300
Boca Raton, FL 33487-2742

© 2004 by Taylor & Francis Group, LLC
CRC Press is an imprint of Taylor & Francis Group, an Informa business

First issued in paperback 2019

No claim to original U.S. Government works

ISBN 13: 978-0-367-44656-7 (pbk)
ISBN 13: 978-1-56881-208-3 (hbk)

Visit the Taylor & Francis Web site at
http://www.taylorandfrancis.com

and the CRC Press Web site at
http://www.crcpress.com

Dedicated to David and Patricia.

Contents

Listings

Preface

This is the second book I have written about Artificial Intelligence (AI) and computer games. My first book was closely based on my PhD thesis and although it was therefore quite specialized it was well received. I was pleased by the compliments I received from some well-known game developers who told me they had enjoyed reading it and found it helpful. This new book is more accessible than the last one and should appeal to an even wider audience. I believe it should be useful to anyone looking to become a game AI programmer, as well as those already working in the field.

I also hope that this book will spark new interest among academics in AI research for computer games. There is a tendency to assume that games are just another application area for AI and as such they deserve no special attention. While it is true that many general purpose AI algorithms are applicable to games, there is also a wealth of opportunity for more specialized study.

There are already several interesting books available that are either solely or partially dedicated to AI and games. Those other books tend to take the form of compendiums of articles by different authors about a wide range of AI-related topics. Instead of trying to compete, in this book I take a complementary approach that presents a more unified overview of AI in games. In particular, the unifying theme of this book is of a Non-Player Character (NPC) and the capabilities that can be built into it.

There are also an enormous number of books on the subject of AI in general. The wonderful thing about the existence of all these books is that it provides such a firm foundation to build upon. There is no need for subsequent books on AI (like this one) to rehash all the same ideas and algorithms. Instead, this book is free to concentrate solely on the application of AI to games and to give references for introductory material that is readily available elsewhere. At the other end of the spectrum, this book also provides a jumping-off point to many advanced topics in AI that are relevant to games.

In this day and age there are also many game- and AI-related resources online that provide lots of detailed information about algorithms and techniques. This book does, of course, contain a comprehensive bibliography that includes some web sites, but a traditional bibliography is limited and soon becomes out of date. There is therefore a companion web site for this book at www.ai4games.org that you will be referred to throughout the text for additional resources and information.

Since my first book, I have been working in the games industry developing AI technology. The experience has given me a much clearer understanding of game AI, and a perspective that I think many academics lack. For example, many academics will make efficiency arguments for why their AI is good for games. But AI programming is not usually such a significant part of the cost of a game that, from a business point of view, it would justify the risk of using a new technique. What the business people in the games industry do care about, however, is new effects that can help differentiate their game from the competition.

Typically new effects have come from the graphics industry, for example, the move to three-dimensions, texture maps, and lately, real-time procedural shading languages. That is why new games are constantly pushing the envelope for graphics while they often languish in the past with their AI. Until AI has some new exciting effects to offer the mainstream game player, this will continue to be the case.

Sooner or later graphics is going to run out of steam as a driving force behind games. Already the law of diminishing returns makes it hard for the casual gamer to tell the difference between this year and last year's graphics. AI has the potential to become the new driving force behind computer game innovation. With the right technology, whole exciting new game genres could be developed. I hope this book will help you think about new AI effects for your games that will generate enthusiasm for AI among game designers and players.

Acknowledgments

I am currently working at a startup which I cofounded that develops AI technology for the entertainment industry. It is one of my hopes that this book, by promoting a common framework and terminology, will make it easier for game developers to interact with AI middleware companies. At the time of writing, we are still being secretive about the technology we have developed so I have been careful not to include any confidential information in the writing of this book. Nevertheless many of my ideas about the general topic of game AI have been shaped and heavily influenced by my experiences at work and by the people with whom I work. I am therefore indebted to many of my current and former colleagues: Brian Cabral, Wolff Dobson, Nigel Duffy, Michael McNally, Ron Musick, Stuart Reynolds, Xiaoyuan Tu (cofounder), Ian Wright, and Wei Yen (CEO and cofounder).

Wei Yen is a remarkable person to whom I am grateful for giving me the opportunity to work for him in such an educational and interesting environment. Ian, Michael, and Wolff have all developed successful commercial games and their experience has been invaluable to me in understanding how AI is applied in the real world of game programming. Ian also proofread the book and provided numerous suggestions on style and content throughout the writing process that have significantly improved the book. Michael has taught me a great deal about programming and about good ways to organize a game's architecture. Ian and Brian have also improved my knowledge of programming. Nigel and Ron have taught me an enormous amount about AI, and Stuart has taught me a lot about reinforcement learning in particular. Xiaoyuan has been at the heart of developing our core technology and has helped me develop a deeper understanding of AI. Dale Schuurmans and Stuart Russell also deserve special mention for it was they who helped provide me with a more modern perspective on AI. Thanks also to Benjamin Funge who helped out with some proofreading.

I have also benefited from numerous conversations with people in the games industry over the years, too many to list, but I am thankful to them too. While much of the credit for the ideas in this book therefore lies with other people, the responsibility for any errors or omissions is obviously my own.

Xiaoyuan is my colleague and also my wife. At home, I am grateful for her love, kindness, and support. On the subject of home, I would also like to express my appreciation to Pung Pung and Willow for their companionship.

Finally, I would like to thank Alice Peters and all the staff at A K Peters for their support, understanding, and encouragement throughout the writing of this book. Special thanks to Jonathan Peters and the people at Garage Games for contributing their time and artwork to produce such a wonderful front cover.

John Funge
Sunnyvale, CA
USA

Chapter 1

Introduction

Computer games, or perhaps more accurately, video games, began with the invention of "Tennis for Two" in 1958. It was not until the 1970s that Atari introduced a wider audience to computer games with the successful console game Pong. Since then computer games have become a multibillion-dollar industry with countless titles published every year. Despite the large number of individual game titles, there is a relatively small set of different game genres. The exact list of genres is debatable, and just like with movies, people argue about which genre(s) a particular game belongs to. This book's companion web site (www.ai4games.org) has links to sites that provide a comprehensive list of genres and example games from each. There are also additional links to interesting information on the history and status of computer games.

1.1 Computer Game Characters

Lara Croft, Mario, and Pac-Man are all well-known computer game characters. Each of them is an example of a *player character*. A player character is a character whose behavior is controlled by a human player through some input device like a joystick. For example, the player presses the A button and the character jumps, presses the B button and it punches, pushes up on the thumb pad and it walks forward, and so on. Player characters often play the hero in a game and *Non-Player Characters* (NPCs) play the other roles such as villains, side-kicks, and cannon-fodder. Wario (Mario's evil brother), Blinky, Pinky, Inky, and Clyde (the four ghosts in Pac-Man) are some rare examples of characters who originally became famous as NPCs.

The distinction between player characters and NPCs is not always straightforward. For example, some games allow the player to control different characters at different times. In such cases, which characters are player characters and which are NPCs is constantly changing. In games where the player controls a party of characters (a team or squad) the switch between player character and NPC can be so fluid that the distinction becomes blurred. That is, the NPCs behave autonomously until the player intercedes to give them a direct order. They then carry out the order, after which they revert to behaving autonomously.

Within a game, NPCs also take on the role of camera person, lighting technician, commentator, and even director. Of course, there is (usually) no little person rendered into the scene who is holding a camera, moving lights around, providing commentary, or directing the other NPCs. There is, however, a piece of code that is controlling the camera, lighting, commentary, direction, etc. It is convenient to think of these pieces of code as NPCs as they share many properties with their on-screen counterparts. Most of techniques in this book therefore apply equally well to NPCs behind the camera as to those in front.

1.2 Behavior

Every character in a game has at least one *controller* associated with it and controllers can be shared between different characters. A controller acts as the character's brain, its inputs are information about the state of the game world, and the outputs are the action choices that affect the game world and produce the associated NPC's behavior.[1]

In other publications, the term "controller" is sometimes used to refer to the player's input device. In this book, "controller" is used exclusively in the sense of the character's brain. The term "joystick" is used for the player's input device.

---

[1]When it is obvious from the context, the term "NPC's associated controller" is often just replaced with "NPC". For example, "the NPC chooses to jump" is understood to mean "the NPC's associated controller chooses to jump".

For player characters the controller consists of a mechanism for interpreting the player's various joystick presses. Of course, the human player's brain is also technically part of the player character's controller because that is where decisions about how to behave originate.

For NPCs the controller can take many forms and have various capabilities. The possible forms and capabilities of an NPC's controller is specifically what this book is all about.

Most players do not care what underlying mechanism is being used to create the appearance, movement, or behavior of the NPCs. The player is simply concerned about the end result. For behavior that means whether the NPCs are behaving "rationally". Rationality has to be defined with respect to what the NPC is trying to achieve because, from a wider perspective, its goals can be irrational. For example, it is not really rational for an NPC to run out from its hiding place and attack the player character who is usually much stronger and has just wiped out all of the NPC's comrades.

An NPC's ultimate goal is to be entertaining, but that goal is usually implicit. Instead, the NPC's controller will have been given lower-level tasks, such as trying to stop the player character at all costs. The tasks are those that the game designer hopes will lead to exciting game play.

What specifically counts as rational depends on the game, the difficulty level the game is being played at, the context within the game, and even the the player's expectations. Nevertheless, there are many common and easily-recognized examples of irrational behavior caused by bugs in a controller, for example, two NPCs continuously butting heads as they both try and go up a ladder at the same time or a battalion of NPCs charging across a battlefield in single file so that they can be easily mowed down by a single machine gunner.

Compared to the capabilities of humans, there are presently a huge number of technical limitations on an NPC's possible capabilities. But since it is only the behavior that counts, the game developer has a great deal of flexibility in choosing which of the possible capabilities a controller, and by extension the associated NPC, should have. Often two similar looking behaviors can be created in completely different ways. For example, consider the problem of getting an NPC to figure out how to get from one location to another. This is called *path planning*. One way to implement path planning is to use a controller that includes a map and a path planning algorithm. This approach is described in detail in Chapter 6. Another approach is to simply have someone (often a level designer) go through and annotate the game world with "signposts". The signposts are not visible to the human player, but the NPC can use them. Whenever an NPC wants to get somewhere its underlying controller simply follows the corresponding signposts. From the player's perspective the behavior of the NPC can seem more or less identical in both cases.

Adding signposts to a map can (depending on the size and complexity of the map) be laborious, time-consuming, and error-prone. Moreover, if the map ever changes, or there are new maps, some or all of the map annotation must be re-generated. In contrast, the path planning approach is general across different maps. It should even work on maps created by the player, for example, a "mod". Nevertheless, the signpost approach is appealing in its simplicity and the high degree of fine-grained control it affords over behavior. It is also less demanding of hardware requirements and programming skills. Both methods are therefore legitimate and each has relative pros and cons that are a microcosm of the often lively debate about which capabilities an NPC really needs.

In general, the answer to the question about what capabilities an NPC's controller must, should, or could have will be determined on a case by case basis. The decision will depend on the capabilities of the underlying hardware, availability of software, level of expertise, familiarity with techniques, and personal preferences.

1.3 Overview

Figure 1.1 is a system architecture diagram for a typical game that shows the major components and their interactions. The architecture is just one possible software architecture. Alternatives will, however, all share roughly the same components. Briefly, the role of each component is:

Game-state. The game-state represents the current state of the world. It knows about all the objects in the world and provides access to them so that they can be queried by all the other components for information about their current state.

Simulator. The simulator encodes the rules of how the game-state changes, i.e. the game's "physics". Together with a set of animations it is the

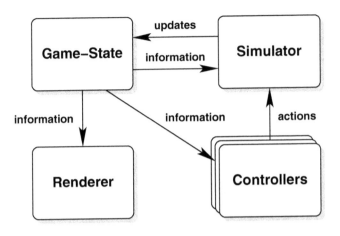

Figure 1.1. Architecture overview.

simulator that is therefore responsible for generating a character's movement in response to the actions chosen by the associated controller.

Renderer. Together with a game's geometry and texture maps, the renderer is responsible for rendering a depiction of the game-state. The output usually consists of images and sounds.

Controllers. Each character in the game has at least one controller associated with it. The controller is responsible for selecting actions. For player characters the controller interprets joystick presses. For NPCs the controller is the AI and low-level control that make up the character's brain.

To be able to influence the game world through its action choices an NPC needs to be embodied in the game. Chapter 2 therefore describes how the the game-state, the simulator, and the controllers work together to enable an NPC to act within the game world.

Just as fundamental as the capability to act in the game, is the ability for an NPC to perceive its world. Otherwise the associated controller cannot know which action is appropriate, or what effect its actions have, and the character is just stumbling around in the dark. For the player character, for which the human is an integral part of the controller, the renderer provides the necessary feedback on what is happening in the game world. NPCs can instead just query the game-state directly to find out the information they need. It is easier, however, to write controllers if the unimportant details (from an AI perspective) can be abstracted away. A more abstract representation emphasizes the crucial similarities between game-states and allows controllers to be written in a more general fashion. Chapter 3 therefore describes some common and useful transformations of information from the game-state, and explains how to limit access to the game-state so an NPC perceives its world in a way that matches the intuitive expectations of the human player more closely.

Once an NPC can perceive its world, it needs to be able to make decisions about how to act. These decisions are contingent on the information it receives. Therefore, Chapter 4 describes how to write *reactive controllers* that can pick actions in reaction to the current perceived state of the game world.

Reactive controllers can be used to create a wide range of useful behavior. But without the ability to remember, controllers can end up going around in circles (literally and figuratively) as they are unable to realize when they have been in a similar situation before. Chapter 5 therefore describes how to add internal state to an NPC's controller that can be used to remember the past. NPCs thus have the capability to make decisions that depend not only on what is currently occurring, but on what occured before. An NPC with a controller that has the capability to remember (an arbitrary amount of) the past and act accordingly can be programmed to perform any computable behavior.[2]

Effective and powerful controllers can be written to achieve their goals by blindly following a set of preprogrammed rules. However, Chapter 6 explains that if a controller is given explicit goals, it can instead automatically search for actions that achieve these goals. To do so, a controller needs access to a model of its world that it can use to predict the outcome of action sequences before it executes them. The model of its world can be provided by giving the controller access to the game simulator. However, it is often sufficient, and faster, just to give a controller an approximate model of its world. Although searching is a powerful technique, it is also one that can consume a lot of CPU and memory resources.

---

[2]This is because it is Turing complete. That is, it is theoretically equivalent to a Turing machine, which is a mathematical model of what it means for something to be computable.

Beyond the simple capability to remember past events, an NPC's controller can also be given the capability to learn from past events. The idea of learning something implies some ability to generalize from past experience to new unseen cases. This is different from simply remembering what happened in the past and regurgitating it. There are many possible ways learning can be used inside controllers; Chapter 7 focuses on how a controller can be automatically learned by trial and error.

By the end of the book you should be able to recognize which techniques might have been used to generate the behavior you see in the computer games you play. You will also be able to decide which capabilities are appropriate for the NPCs in your game. Together with the references, and online resources available from this book's companion web site, you should also be able to implement controllers for NPCs with the capabilities you choose.

There are many other capabilities, not covered in this book, that an NPC's controller could be given. For example, if an NPC had access to a camera that looked out upon a game player's world it could be given the capability to see. With a microphone, the capability to understand and generate speech also becomes important. Cameras and microphones are an as yet small but growing part of computer games (see [Mar01, LDG03]).

1.4 Artificial Intelligence

Many of the potential capabilities of an NPC's controller are made possible thanks to the academic field of AI. AI began as a research field in the 1940s. There were some early successes and this led to great optimism about how quickly computers could become as intelligent as humans. Researchers, however, soon realized that many AI problems were much harder than they first appeared. In the 1980s expert systems emerged as a knowledge based approach to solving AI problems. The idea behind an expert system is that the knowledge of human experts is encoded into a Knowledge Base (KB). The KB can then be used to answer questions and solve problems.

Expert systems have had many well-known successes both in the academic and commercial world. They do, however, suffer from the serious drawback of having to create a KB that can cover all possible cases in advance. The problem with creating a KB is that the amount of knowledge required to solve even simple problems can be enormous. Creating the KB can therefore be time-consuming, expensive, and error-prone. This has led to the criticism that expert systems are brittle and only applicable to so-called "toy problems".

To reduce the size of the required KB, logical reasoning (and the closely related subject of planning) have been widely studied throughout the history of AI. The idea is that logical consequences of the KB can be inferred rather than represented explicitly. For example, a KB might contain "All plumbers have mustaches" and that "Mario is a plumber", but not explicitly "Mario has a mustache". Instead, a reasoning engine can use logical deduction to answer "yes" to the question: "Does Mario have a mustache?" There are two criticisms that are commonly leveled at logical reasoning: first, for propositional logic there are problems that require an exponential amount of time to solve and for first-order logic there are problems that are uncomputable; and second, that the real world contains much uncertainty but logical inference is better suited to dealing with precise mathematical concepts.

A breakthrough in expert systems that addresses the uncertainty present in the real world has been the development of so called *graphical models*. Bayes nets and Hidden Markov Models (HMMs) are two well-known examples of graphical models. Efficient algorithms for probabilistic reasoning have been developed for graphical models and they have been successfully applied to many real-world problems like medical diagnosis and spam filtering. They are a manifestation of an important and well-established trend in modern AI research to use mathematical probability as the correct way to handle uncertainty.

When many labeled examples of a problem exist (or can be generated), an alternative to manually creating a KB is to create one automatically. Automatically acquiring knowledge is the domain of machine learning. Machine learning has a long tradition in AI, but many of the early approaches lacked firm theoretical underpinnings and neglected the importance of real-world empirical results. In contrast, a great anecdote that demonstrates the promise of modern statistical machine learning to automatically create useful KBs is provided by the FlipDog[TM] story. FlipDog was founded in 2000 as a spin-off from WhizBang! Labs[TM]. FlipDog used machine learning techniques to allow their webbot to learn to recognize job postings on the Internet. The webbot then trawled the Web and in less than a year acquired over 600,000 jobs from more than 50,000 employers in more than 3,500 locations. FlipDog was set to quickly eclipse the older and more established Monster.com™ as the market leader. Monster.com had been relying on more conventional means to build a KB of job postings. Monster.com quickly realized that FlipDog represented the future and acquired the company for an undisclosed sum.

The standard reference on AI is [RN02]; it has clear, incisive, and in-depth coverage on most of the important areas of AI. What that book does not cover, and what this book therefore focuses on, is the application of AI to games. Nevertheless, it is inevitable that this book must frequently venture into AI topics not specific to games. On those occasions (unless there is something specific to add) this book provides references, but does not attempt to go over the same material.

1.5 Game AI

The term "game AI" is sometimes used to distinguish AI used in computer games from academic AI. In particular, AI used in computer games does not have to be general purpose. The goal is not (necessarily) to advance human understanding by writing a technical paper. Often a solution is acceptable as long as a character's behavior appears to be plausible over some narrow range of situations. There are, however, clear economic advantages to generating solutions that are as general as possible.

The ease with which some problems could be solved in unconventional ways led to some initial misplaced optimism about the prospects of AI in games. For example, some people were led to make bold claims that AI techniques derived from games would soon surpass the capabilities of academic AI. It is interesting to note that in the early days of AI research similar enthusiasm was expressed by academics who were buoyed by their early successes on toy problems.

Aside from the degree of required generality, another disconnect between game AI and academic AI is the scope of what is considered AI. In particular, academic AI often has a different focus than game AI and there is an adage that once an AI problem is solved, it is no longer considered AI. Game AI is often used to refer to any kind of control problem in a game, some of which are more traditionally in the domain of control theory. For example, trying to figure out the joint angles so that a character's hand moves to a specified point is sometimes thought to be a game AI problem. Outside of games it would be recognized as an inverse kinematics problem that has been well studied in robotics and control theory. This book emphasizes the problem of generating higher-level behavior, more in line with the traditional academic use of the term AI. There are numerous books on control theory that the interested reader can consult. A classic reference is [DB04]. There are also many papers on the application of control theory and AI techniques to low-level control problems in game-like worlds; see [GT95, HP97, LvdPF00, FvdPT01, LCR03].

The typical approach to creating high-level behavior in games can be largely characterized as the brute force approach of creating a controller that contains lots of knowledge about how to behave. This corresponds to building a controller that is an expert system; a game-specific expert system for deciding what the NPC should do next. As an expert system, the controller will suffer from all the scalability problems that plague expert systems in general, which often manifests itself as brittle AI. In particular, the enormous task of trying to anticipate all the situations that might arise inevitably means that some (possibly many) possibilities get overlooked. When one of the unanticipated situations does arise the NPC behaves inappropriately and can end up looking stupid.

If an AI bug is noticed in time it can be fixed by adding a new bit of knowledge to tell the controller what to do in the previously unanticipated situation. This gets to the heart of why expert systems can be problematic. The real world is so complicated that this process of adding new knowledge is potentially neverending. Only in toy problems is there any reasonable hope of finishing the task. That is why the expert system approach can be, and has been, successful in games. Many game worlds are, by definition, toy problems. If the game world is simple enough an expert system might therefore be appropriate. Games also have the advantage that the AI does not have to be perfect. The game can probably ship when the process of adding more knowledge offers diminishing returns. If there are still a few infrequent AI bugs then, provided they are not too glaring and it does not affect the overall enjoyment of the game, no one will mind. The same cannot be said of an AI medical diagnosis program!

Nevertheless, as game worlds become ever more sophisticated and less toy-like, the expert system approach will struggle to keep pace. To date, machine learning has only been used sporadically in computer games. But as games become more complex, machine learning techniques will enable the AI to scale up and will inevitably become more commonplace.

In contrast to learning, search is often used in existing computer games. The special case of searching for a path to a given location (i.e., path planning) is particularly widespread, but as explained in Chapter 6, the same basic technology can also be employed to achieve a wide range of behaviors.

There are (usually) no inherently noisy sensors in a game world, but there are other sources of uncertainty. For example, uncertainty can be artificially added to increase realism (see Section 3.4 in Chapter 3) and there is inherent uncertainty about future states of the game world (see Section 3.5 in Chapter 3). Therefore some of the techniques, like graphical models, that were developed to deal with real-world uncertainty are potentially applicable to computer games. In particular, graphical models could be used to create expert systems that are less brittle and better able to handle uncertainty. Graphical models are also an important representation used for some learning algorithms. However, if the graphical model is only effectively removing uncertainty artificially added to increase realism, then there is clearly no net benefit.

There are some existing books about AI for games; see [Fun99, Cha03]. There are also a number of compendiums of articles by various authors that (among other subjects) cover a wide range of game AI-related topics: [DeL00, DeL01, TD02, Kir04, Rab02, Rab03a]. There is even a web site that attempts to catalog every game AI-related article [Rab03b]. Whenever there is a potential overlap, and there is nothing to add, this book avoids repeating information found in these other sources by providing references.

1.5.1 Game Design

The underlying technology is only one factor that influences the quality of the AI in a game; in some games the AI task is simply harder. Games can, however, sometimes be designed or modified to make life easier for the AI component. For example, the camera can be brought closer to the player character so that fewer NPCs are on screen at any one time.

Often in games a relatively simple controller can still yield complex behavior. For example, Section 4.2 in Chapter 4 explains how if each NPC follows just a few simple rules it can give rise to sophisticated flocking behavior among a group of NPCs. This phenomenon of a few local rules giving rise to interesting global behavior is known as *emergence* and many games take advantage of it.[3] Typically the possibility space is so large that it is hard to control or anticipate exactly what behavior will emerge. In some games this is a big bonus as the game experience continues to evolve in ways the game designer might never have imagined. In other more tightly scripted games it can be viewed as a problem and game designers might shy away from using controllers with a large possibility space. But from an AI perspective restricting the possibility space can be a challenge and the resulting code is usually full of special cases, which make it buggy and hard to maintain.

By way of analogy, a good anecdote about the trade-off between controller simplicity and the level of control over the resulting behavior is nicely illustrated by a story from the computer animation industry. The director in an animation wanted a scene with raindrops rolling down a window, so the animators built an elegant program that generated the desired animation procedurally. The director was initially delighted when he saw the realistic-looking results that had been produced so quickly. But he was a perfectionist and on close examination he became unhappy with the precise movement of some of the raindrops. Of course, the programmers had no control over the animation at that level of detail, they simply set the initial conditions and let the simulation run autonomously. They could generate realistic-looking animations, but they could not generate (except by trial and error) the precise realistic-looking animation the director was after. The program was scrapped and the raindrop animation was created instead by hours of painstaking work animating the scene by hand. The connection with games is that in some games it is desirable to have realistic-looking behavior emerge from an elegant controller, but in some games the game designer might require more control.

In terms of the player's perception of a game's AI, appropriate animations can also make an enormous difference. For example, consider an NPC who is surrounded by hostile monsters and cannot think of anything intelligent to do. The NPC could simply stand there looking dumb, or the animation system can be triggered to play an animation of the NPC running around screaming. It is surprising how an appropriate animation can

---

[3] See [Wol02] for a fascinating look at the properties of emergence in an abstract mathematical setting.

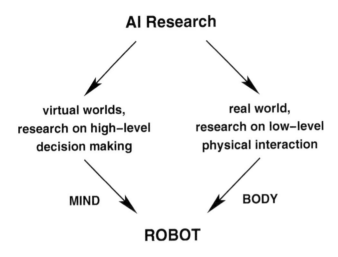

Figure 1.2. Different research tracks within AI.

make all the difference in the player's perception of the AI.

In summary, extensive play testing often shows up situations that were not anticipated by the AI programmer. If the AI bug is something simple it can be fixed by changing the controller. This section makes it clear that changing the game design, or simply playing an appropriate animation, can also sometimes provide a work-around.

1.5.2 Computer Games and AI Research

One of the major goals of AI research is to produce intelligent robots. Figure 1.2 shows that creating a robot is (at least) a two-pronged effort. For a time, there was a push in AI not to work on the high-level decision-making aspect until the low-level physical interaction research program was further along [Bro90]. But as pointed out in [Etz93] the two endeavors can obviously be worked on in parallel. Computer games therefore make a wonderful medium for carrying out research into abstract thinking. Of course, simulated worlds have been used before in AI, but computer games offer a commercial application with a degree of visual feedback in an intuitive real-time environment that is hard to match.

Until the physical interaction research program is further along, doing research on abstract thinking in the real world can mean a lot of wasted time dealing with problems like faulty actuators and uncalibrated sensors.

That is why AI research in robotics often ends up with applications like a robot trundling around picking up soda cans. As mechanical engineering improves more exciting applications are opening up, but computer games still offer an exciting and easily accessible platform for AI research.

Computer games even have something to offer the physical interaction research program. For example, in [TR97] a game-like world is rendered from the point of view of each eye of an NPC and vision algorithms are applied to the resulting pair of stereoscopic images. The end result of the vision algorithms could be obtained more quickly and easily by using the original three-dimensional representation of the world before it is rendered. However, the point of the exercise is not the end result, but to use the convenience of a game world to test and develop algorithms that could be used in the real world.

Chapter 2

Acting

This chapter describes how the AI in a character's controller interacts with the rest of the game. Although not specifically about AI, it is nonetheless important as it introduces an underlying game architecture that embodies a character's controller within the game. The controller can then perform actions to influence its world, which, along with the ability to perceive its world (covered in the next chapter), is one of the most basic capabilities it needs.

Recall from Chapter 1 that the game architecture is broken down into the game-state, the simulator, and the controllers. Each of these components is described in turn, but first this chapter introduces a simple game that is used as a motivating example throughout the rest of the book.

2.1 Tag Game

Since the game-state and simulator are different for each game it is difficult to describe them in completely general terms. Therefore they are introduced in the context of a specific example game: a simple game of tag.

Figure 2.1 depicts a scene from the tag game. The scene is depicted in three dimensions but all the important movement in the tag game takes place on a two-dimensional plane. This is often referred to as $2\frac{1}{2}D$.

The tag game begins with one character chosen at random to be the tagged character. The tagged character then chases the other characters until it touches one. Once a new character has been touched it takes over the role of the tagged character and the game continues. Either NPCs or

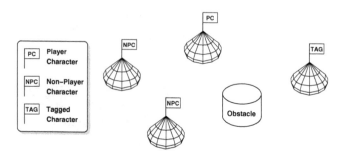

Figure 2.1. Scene from the tag game.

player characters can take on the role of the tagged character. To make the game a little more interesting there are some obstacles placed randomly within the game world.

By the standards of modern computer games, the tag game is hopelessly simple. Nevertheless, from an AI perspective it possesses many of the important characteristics of a more complicated game. The basic architecture should therefore apply to other games, while the simplicity makes it free of unimportant and distracting details that might encumber a more realistic example.

To help make the details of code organization within the tag game clearer, C++ is used to provide declarations for some of the important classes. Appendix B contains a few notes about the use of C++ within this book, and about game programming in general. You might therefore want to look at the relevant pages before proceeding.

2.2   Game-State

The game-state is the object that provides access to a complete description of the current state of the game world. Listing 2.1 shows part of the declaration of the tgGameState class. Only a few sample methods and class members are shown, but hopefully they show how the game-state provides access to a complete description of the state of the game world. That is, there are accessors for all game objects the game-state manages and those in turn provide accessors to their state information. For example, to find

```
class tgGameState
{
public:
    tgGameState();
    ~tgGameState();
    // Get the number of objects
    inline int getNumObjects() const;
    // Get a pointer to ith object
    inline tgObject* getObject(int i);
    // Get the number of characters
    inline int getNumCharacters() const;
    // Get a pointer to the ith character
    // NOTE: not necessarily the same as the ith object
    inline tgCharacter* getCharacter(int i);
    // Get the current time
    inline tgReal getTime() const;
    // Adopt an object
    void addObject(tgObject* o);
private:
    // List of all game objects
    vector<tgObject*> objects;
    // The current time
    tgReal time;
}; // tgGameState
```

Listing 2.1. Part of the game-state class declaration.

out from the game-state the current velocity of the *i* th character use:

```
// gs is the game-state object
tgRealVec const& v = gs.getCharacter(i)->getVelocity();
```

The base class for all the objects in the game is the tgObject class. Listing 2.2 contains part of the class declaration. Once again only a small representative sample of the available methods and member variables is shown.

NPCs and player characters are both instances of the tgCharacter class, a part of which is shown in Listing 2.3. The tgCharacter is a subclass of a tgObstacle class (not shown) that defines the physical extent of an object used in collision detection. The tgObstacle class is itself a subclass of the tgObject class.

Instances of NPCs and players are created as part of the program initialization:

```
// Shared perception object (see Chapter 3)
tgPerception perception(&gs);
for (int i = 0; i < numCharacters; i++)
{
    tgCharacter* c = NULL;
    if (0 == i)
    { // make character 0 the player character
        c = new tgCharacter(&gs, new tgControllerPC(&perception));
    }
    else
    {
        c = new tgCharacter(&gs, new tgControllerNPC(&perception));
    }
    gs.addObject(c);
}
```

As you can see, the only difference between NPCs and player characters is they have different types of controller. By swapping in different types of controllers a character can be either a player character or an NPC. The ability to swap controllers is useful for games where players can flip between characters to control. It is also important for testing because the game can be played without human intervention for hours on end to try and find bugs that might not show up during regular play testing.

2.3 Simulator

The simulator is responsible for making changes to the game-state. Ideally, the simulator is the *only* component of the game that can modify the game-state. All other components can only query the game-state.

```
class tgObject
{
public:
    tgObject(tgGameState* gs);
    virtual ~tgObject();
    // Get this object's position
    inline tgRealVec const& getPosition() const;
    // Set this object's position
    inline void setPosition(tgRealVec const& pos);
    // Get this object's mass
    inline tgReal const& getMass() const;
    // Set this object's mass
    inline void setMass(tgReal const& mass);
protected:
    // Local pointer to the game–state used in various methods
    // to access information about other objects in the game
    tgGameState* gs;
private:
    // This object's position
    tgRealVec pos;
    // This object's mass
    tgReal mass;
}; // tgObject
```

Listing 2.2. Part of the declaration of the base class for all objects in the game.

Action choices, the passage of time, and game world events like collisions are common causes of modifications to the game-state. The rules contained in the simulator that determine how to modify the game-state represent the game world's physics. Game physics obviously do not have to obey the same physical laws as the real world.

Note that, the separation of the simulator from the renderer is important if, as in Chapter 6, the simulator is used by an NPC as a world model to think about the consequences of its actions. Otherwise an NPC just thinking ahead would change what the player sees on the screen.

```
class tgCharacter : public tgObstacleCircle
{
public:
    tgCharacter(tgGameState* gs, tgController* controller);
    ~tgCharacter();
    // Get this character's controller
    inline tgController* getConstroller();
    // Set this character's controller
    inline void setController(tgController* controller);
    // Get this character's velocity
    inline tgRealVec const& getVelocity();
    // Set this character's velocity
    inline void setVelocity(tgRealVec const& vel);
private:
    // Pointer to this character's (possibly shared) controller
    tgController* controller;
    // This character's velocity
    tgRealVec vel;
};
```

Listing 2.3. Part of the class declaration for characters in the game.

2.3.1 Actions

A character's controller is responsible for selecting actions, but it is the simulator's job to resolve the effects of actions on the game-state. Often the immediate effects of an action are followed by additional ramifications. For example, activating an explosive device might be instantaneous, but the subsequent explosion could cause all sorts of ripple effects. Fortunately, the simulator can be written to deal with the effects one at a time. For instance, in the example of an explosion, the initial act of activating the explosive device causes the simulator to set the explosive device to "on". After some amount of predefined time the explosive device controller generates an explode action. This causes the simulator to play animations of explosions and characters being flung around. This might result in the death of a character that was some NPC's friend. This in turn causes the corresponding NPC's controller to, say, choose a shoot action aimed at the character who set the explosion. The shoot action is then resolved by the simulator, and so on.

Although the simulator processes events one at a time, it can of course alternate between different tasks. Since it all happens so fast, events often appear to be happening simultaneously and in parallel.

Action Representation

One of the first steps in creating a game is to decide what actions are available and how they are represented. The decision can depend upon the complexity of the game world's physics. For example, in a simple world a "drop" action could just mean an object is deleted from the character's inventory and placed back into the world at a nearby location. At the other end of the spectrum, a game might simulate some of the laws of physics found in the real world. In such a world a character could have an action to relax its muscles. This then sets in motion a chain of events such as the force that was previously holding the object in place disappearing. The force of gravity then automatically starts accelerating the object toward the floor. This in turn causes a collision event between the object and the floor to be generated, and so on. In most games, the physics are somewhere in between these two extremes. But deciding on the correct level of abstraction, particularly between controllers and motion-captured animations, is a difficult problem.

The representation of actions is also complicated by the fact that actions can sometimes be parameterized. For example, a punch action might have a parameter indicating how hard to punch.

2.3.2 Animations

Animations are sometimes thought of as the renderer's responsibility. This might be because they are often created by the same artists who create the texture maps and three-dimensional models that are used by the renderer. Motion capture is another common source of animations. Regardless of an animation's genesis, while it is playing it is providing rules for how the associated object should move. In general, it is the simulator that encodes the rules on how an object should move. It makes sense therefore to think of animations as implicitly encoding part of the game's physics as animation data and for them to be managed by the simulator.

Animations are triggered by actions and events that occur in the game world. When an animation is triggered the simulator proceeds to step through the animation. This continues until the animation is interrupted or completed. The current animation often needs to be interrupted by events, such as collisions, or new actions selected by a controller. When an animation is interrupted a new animation often needs to take its place. Blending between the current and the requested animation can require the simulator to modify one or both of the animations on the fly. Modification of an animation can consist of dropping frames to speed it up, or rescaling to make a smoother blend (see [KGP02]). Section 2.5.1 describes subtle interactions that can arise between the simulator and a controller when trying to smoothly blend between animations.

Note that, creating motion capture data requires careful planning to make sure a full and complete set of animations is obtained [Kin00]. But no matter how many animations are captured they will usually still need to be modified at runtime. The reason is that control generally needs to be exerted at a higher frequency than can be provided by a discrete fixed set of available animations.

2.3.3 Newtonian Physics

Except at speeds approaching the velocity of light, Newtonian physics provides an accurate model for movement in the real world. It is not surprising therefore that many games incorporate some aspect of Newtonian physics into the simulator in order to generate realistic-looking motions.

One of the biggest challenges with incorporating Newtonian physics into a game is that for active objects (like NPCs) locomotion can become a difficult control problem. Therefore Newtonian physics is most commonly applied to passive objects (ones with no internal source of energy). Some good references for Newtonian physics and games are [Bou01, WB01]. A few representative papers on tackling the control problem associated with the use of Newtonian physics for active objects are [GT95, HP97, LvdPF00, FvdPT01, LCR03].

In some popular cartoons an interesting version of Newtonian physics is used in which the law of gravity fails to apply until the character realizes it has run off the edge of a cliff. As suggested in [Fal95], there is no reason why simulators in games could not incorporate such imaginative variations on Newtonian physics for the purposes of entertainment.

2.3.4 Tag Game Physics

The physics in the tag game uses a two-dimensional version of the *simple vehicle model* described in [Rey99] and originally inspired by [Bra84]. The vehicle model approximates the Newtonian physics of a vehicle with a point mass. The term "vehicle" is used loosely to apply to a wide variety of objects, to quote from [Rey99]:

> ... from wheeled devices to horses, from aircraft to submarines, and (while certainly stretching the terminology) to include lo-comotion by a character's own legs.

In the case of the tag game, the vehicle refers to a character in the game.

Actions in the tag game are specified in terms of some new desired velocity. The desired velocity is then used to calculate a character's new velocity as follows:

```
// get character c's desired velocity
tgRealVec acceleration(c->getAction().getDesiredVelocity());
acceleration.clamp(c->getMaxForce());
// acceleration = force/mass
acceleration.scale(1.0/c->getMass());
// v = character c's current velocity
tgRealVec v(c->getVelocity());
v.add(acceleration);
v.clamp(c->getMaxSpeed());
c->setVelocity(v);
v.normalize();
c->setOrientation(v);
```

Once a character's new velocity has been determined, its new position is (assuming there are no collisions) just the new velocity added to the previous position:

```
tgCharacter* c = gs->getCharacter(i);
tgRealVec p(c->getPosition());
p.add(c->getVelocity());
c->setPosition(p);
```

One of the most visually obvious defects with the simple vehicle model is that there is no constraint on the rate of turning. In a Newtonian physics simulation this corresponds to moments of inertia. You can approximate the effect of moments of inertia by placing a constraint on rate of turning. But note that this constraint represents an upper bound and it should always be possible to turn less than the maximum turn rate. Otherwise unsightly oscillations can occur when the orientation gets close to the desired one.

2.3.5   Passage of Time

The simulator works by updating the game-state at discrete time intervals. The update frequency can either be a fixed constant as in Section 2.3.7, or allowed to vary as in Section 2.3.8. Regardless of whether the update frequency is allowed to vary, it should be greater than or equal to the frame rate, where the *frame rate* of a game is how many times a second the current state of the world is rendered as an image that is displayed on the screen for the player to see.

Some reasons the update frequency might need to be higher than the frame rate is to avoid missing collisions, or numerically solve stiff differential equations in a complex physical simulation. The frame rate, in turn, needs to be high enough and have low enough variance that motion does not appear jerky and discontinuous. The human eye usually starts to perceive motion as smooth at around 15–20 frames per second. But games that run at 60 Hz still appear a lot smoother than those that run at 30 Hz. Updates to the game-state also need to coincide with frame boundaries or the game will be out of sync.

The simulator still needs to modify the game-state even when no other actions are generated from any of the characters in the game. For example, any active animations still need to continue playing; simulated forces like gravity can cause objects to start or continue accelerating; other objects might have momentum that keeps them moving forward from previous frames; and simulated friction could cause objects to slow down.

2.3.6 Collisions

As objects move around according to the game world's physics they may
bump into each other. Bumping into things can be accidental or deliberate. For example, in the tag game the goal of the tagged character is to
"bump into" another character. The simulator therefore needs to be able
to detect when collisions have occurred. It might also need to be able to
detect when objects are on a collision course even if they have not yet col-
lided. Collision detection is a widely studied problem in many different
research communities. For collision detection in games, see [vdB03] or
any of the other references and resources available on this book's companion web site.

Once a collision has been detected it needs to be resolved. For collisions stemming from deliberate actions, like the tagged character tagging
another character, this usually involves playing a suitable animation. In
addition, the game-state needs to be updated with important information
like the identity of the newly tagged character.

In general, a game's realism is greatly enhanced if the laws of physics
for collisions in the real world can be simulated. This is called *collision
resolution* and there are two common approaches: impulse methods and
penalty methods. See [WB01] and [Bou01] for an in-depth look at collision resolution.

In some games, characters can "collide" with permeable substances
like water, in which case the result of the collision could be that a character
is moving in a different medium. This would presumably require a new set
of appropriate physics rules to be used.

2.3.7 Fixed Time-Step Simulation

In a fixed time-step simulation the game-state is updated at some constant
fixed time interval. Every n time-steps the simulator polls each character's
associated controller to see if there are any actions to execute. In the simplest case $n = 1$ and new actions can be generated every time-step but,
depending on the game, it is usually sufficient to set $n > 1$. The simulator
can also implement time slicing by varying n on a per controller basis. The
order of polling controllers always needs to be randomized or else some
characters are consistently able to act first, while others always act with
the knowledge of the preceding character's choices.

The simulator creates the game-state according to rules that often specify change in a continuous way. Fixed time-step simulation corresponds to sampling the continuously changing state of the game world at fixed intervals. With any fixed sampling technique, events that occur in between samples will go unnoticed. For example, it is quite easy for the simulator to miss collisions and joystick presses. The player, however, may well notice that two objects just seemed to pass through each other in a completely unrealistic fashion, or that their presses are being ignored.

Even when a collision is detected at a particular time-step, it is unlikely the collision occurred at just that instant. Therefore the collision resolution strategy will have to be able to deal with the objects already interpenetrating. This is not such a problem for penalty methods, but could be an issue for impulse methods. In particular, the simulation might need to back up to find the exact time of collision.

It is always possible to construct pathological examples when using a fixed time-step simulation. But in practice, if the update frequency is high enough, then missed events are (probably) rare and (probably) hardly noticeable. A fixed time-step simulator might not be suitable for engineering applications that require a high degree of precision, but for games their simplicity makes them appealing.

2.3.8 Discrete Event Simulation

Discrete event simulation formalizes the notion of an *event*. There are different types of events and each event object has a time associated with it. Events also contain any other relevant information, such as the participants in a collision. Events are stored in a priority queue called the *event queue*, which is sorted by the time of the events. The simulator works by continually popping events off the front of the queue and processing them.

When an event is processed, the game world is simulated up to the time associated with the event. To ensure that an up-to-date version of the game-state is available for the renderer at frame boundaries, special tick events are inserted into the event queue. In particular, when the game starts, the tick event that corresponds to the first frame is placed in the event queue. Subsequently, whenever a tick event is popped from the event queue with associated time t, another tick event is immediately inserted into the event queue with associated time $t' = t + \Delta t$. Note that, to avoid the accumulation of rounding errors the new time t' should not be calculated directly from the previous time. Instead, $t' = n\Delta t$, where n is the (integer) number of tick events so far.

Actions are handled by querying controllers in response to "get action" events that are placed in the queue at appropriate times. Again the query order needs to be randomized and this can be done by shuffling "get action" events that occur at the same time. Instead of just polling each controller at regular intervals, a controller can provide an estimate for how long it needs to calculate an action and insert an appropriate "get action" event in the event queue. Time-slicing for controllers can also be handled easily by scheduling start and stop thinking events that get sent to the respective controllers at appropriate times.

Discrete event simulation provides an elegant way to avoid missing collisions. After each change to the game-state there is a potential for new collisions. A collision detection algorithm is used to find such events and the time at which they occur. The information is then placed in the event queue. When a collision event is popped from the event queue a check is made to see if it is still valid and, if necessary, the collision is then resolved. The validity check is needed because other preceding events (for example, a character changed direction to avoid a collision) may have caused a predicted collision not to occur after all.

2.4 Controllers

Controllers are responsible for selecting the actions that get sent to the simulator. Listing 2.4 shows the tgController class that is the abstract base class for all controllers in the tag game. New controllers are subclasses of tgController and they must implement the calcAction method. As explained in the previous section, the simulator intermittently requests actions from characters' associated controllers. More specifically, the simulator calls a controller's calcAction method and a new action is computed and stored in the action class variable. The computed action can then be retrieved at any point by a call to the getAction method. Ideally, the action class variable should always contain a valid action, if not necessarily a sensible one. Therefore, if a controller cannot, or does not want to compute a new action, it should leave the lastAction variable unchanged, or overwrite it with some valid default value.

```
class tgController
{
public:
    tgController(tgPerception* perception);
    virtual ~tgController();
    // Calculate action for character[myIndex]
    virtual void calcAction(int const myIndex) = 0;
    // Get the last computed action
    inline tgAction const& getAction() { return this->action; }
protected:
    // The controller's perception object (see Chapter 3)
    tgPerception* perception;
    // The last calculated action
    tgAction action;
}; // tgController
```

Listing 2.4. Part of the controller base class declaration.

Every character will have at least one controller associated with it. One reason that a character would have more than one controller associated with it is if it alternates between being an NPC and a player character. Controllers can also be shared among several characters. The myIndex argument passed to the calcAction is the game-state index of the character for which the controller is currently computing an action. This information is also important for the perception object described in the next chapter.

Of course, if a controller is shared it does not mean that all the associated characters will behave in lock step with one another. At any given moment two characters with the same controller will generally be in different situations, so even if their controllers are the same, their behavior can be different. For example, in the tag game one character might be being chased by the tagged character and so is running away, while a different character is standing still hiding behind an obstacle. If the hidden character is spotted and the tagged player comes too close, it too will run away (although from a different starting point and most likely in a different direction).

Even if characters do not share the same controller instance, they can still share the same type of controller. This is often the case with parameterized controllers. For example, a "braveness" parameter could be used as a threshold in a test to decide whether to run away or not. The same controller type can then yield different behavior by instantiating it with different parameter values.

2.4.1 Hierarchical Control

A controller class will often provide other methods that implement what can be thought of as subcontrollers. The calcAction method then acts as the master controller that knows how and when to call the other subcontroller methods to compute an action. The subcontroller methods are usually in the protected section so that they are not publicly available, but can still be used and overridden by subclasses. This allows controllers to be conveniently layered to form hierarchies. At the low-level there are controllers to perform basic tasks like collision avoidance and path following. At the next level could be controllers to plan paths, and higher up still might be controllers that determine NPC motivations and intentions.

A common example of hierarchical control is when the player clicks on a point in the world where the player character should go. The decision on where to go has been made by the player, but getting there is achieved autonomously. The controller that gets a character to a given goal position can be shared by NPCs and player characters. For player characters the goal is provided by the player, but the NPC has the additional task of figuring out where to go and so there must be another controller for this task.

The camera character in many games is an interesting hybrid between a player character and an NPC. For example, some games feature automatic camera control, but it is not fully automatic because what the camera is pointing at has to depend on properties of the world like the player character's position and orientation. Other games allow tighter control over the camera, but usually only over some subset of the camera's degrees of freedom with the remaining ones determined automatically.

2.4.2 Hierarchical Actions

If there is a hierarchy of controllers, there will usually also be a hierarchy of actions. The actions that finally get sent to the simulator are called the *game actions*. Actions that are not game actions, which are generated by high-level controllers, provide part of the input (along with relevant information about the game world) to low-level controllers. The low-level controllers translate the high-level actions into lower-level actions and eventually into game actions. Thus some of the controllers take actions output from other controllers as input. Of course, an "action" output from some controller might just be a numerical parameter input into another controller. Conversely, it could also be a complex behavior that generates a whole sequence of lower-level actions.

Some of the controllers described in Chapter 6 can use the simulator to search for an action to pick by trying out prospective candidates before selecting one. To speed up the search, other controllers might only perform an internal approximate simulation. For example, humans use a simple naive physics model all the time in their everyday lives.

An approximate simulator can even be defined as a separate distinct object that can then be used by any controllers that quickly want to try out actions in advance. The approximate simulator will normally not take game actions as input, but some higher level approximation. For example, in the tag game, the game actions are two-dimensional direction vectors. These could be approximated by discrete compass directions for input into an approximate simulator that represented the world as a two-dimensional grid. Or a discrete graph could be overlaid onto the map as in Section 6.4 in Chapter 6.

Figure 2.2 shows a possible hierarchy of controllers, simulators, and actions for a simple path planning example. The high-level controller decides on some high-level intention such as moving to a far-away location. It then generates a high-level action that consists of a goal location consistent with the intention. A path-planner then generates a sequence of grid locations that form a collision-free path to the goal location. To do this it takes advantage of an approximate simulator that implements movement on a grid as a simplified version of movement in the game. Finally, a path-follower translates the discrete path into a smooth one and sends the game-level actions to the simulator to be executed.

In general, so-called *hybrid controllers* can have highly sophisticated architectures with interrupts and many levels of subcontrollers. There may even need to be an overarching controller that acts as a miniature operating system allocating resources and scheduling other controllers. The *agent*

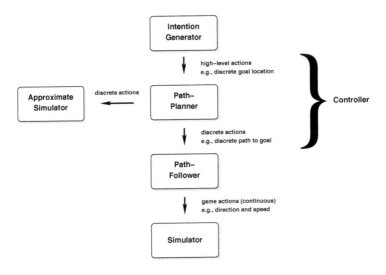

Figure 2.2. Example of a hierarchy of controllers and actions.

architecture literature studies many of these issues in detail. Other sources of inspiration on complex controller architectures are animal and human psychology.

2.4.3 Level of Detail

In computer graphics it is common to use lower resolution textures and simpler geometry when objects are far away from the camera. An analogous idea can be applied to controllers. In particular, an NPC can have a hierarchy of associated controllers that all perform the same task. This is different from the hierarchy of controllers described before because previously each controller performed a different subtask. Although all the controllers perform the same task, controllers higher up the hierarchy are more sophisticated. Some reasons to prefer using simpler controllers lower down in the hierarchy are as follows.

Failure. A more sophisticated controller might occasionally fail to pick an action. This might happen if the algorithm that it uses is specialized to apply only in a narrow range of circumstances. Or it might simply run out of time, or anticipate in advance that there is not enough time. Whatever the reason, a simpler, more reliable controller can be used as a backup.

Distance. If an NPC is far away from the camera, it might be possible to use a simpler controller so that closer NPCs have extra time to use more sophisticated controllers. Unlike the level of detail used in graphics, distance is not always a good measure of the importance of behavior. For example, a general might be far away but could still be in close communciation with her troops. In which case, even though the troops might be closer, it might be sensible to devote more of the available CPU resources to the general's decision making.

Groups. If an NPC is part of a group, then the group itself can be treated as a single entity. For example, if the group's controller decides the group as a whole should move to a particular location, then the individual NPCs within the group need only decide how to get there. If the group later disbands, then the individual NPCs may need to use a more sophisticated controller to determine not just how to get there but where to go in the first place.

2.4.4 Game Action Compatibility

Controllers for player characters have to select game actions according to the player's button presses and joystick pushes. Sometimes this is quite easy and can be accomplished by a simple look-up table. For example, when the player presses the A button the player character controller generates a "punch" action, say. Other times the mapping can be more complicated. For example, generating combos usually requires monitoring the time and frequency of button pushes. Pressure-sensitive input can also be used to provide parameters to actions like how hard to punch.

If an NPC's controller generates actions at the level of button presses and joystick pushes, then its output needs to be filtered through the player character's controller to turn it into game actions. The advantage of having the NPC's controller work this way is that it can greatly simplify the task of swapping controllers and creating automatic tests for debugging the game.

2.5 Possible Actions

Not all the actions that are defined in a game are always possible. For example, a "shoot" action is not possible if a character does not have a gun. If a controller does select an action that is not possible, then executing it could cause the game to crash, or the game-state might become corrupt, leading to bugs and a possible crash later on. Therefore the simulator needs to check if an action is possible and ignore the illegal ones. It also wastes time when an NPC's controller spends time trying to decide whether to select an action that is not even possible. It is therefore a good idea if a controller can have access to information contained within the simulator about which actions are currently possible.

In simple games, where the list of actions is discrete and small, the information about possible actions can be given as an explicit list of actions. In games where actions take parameters, the list of possible actions needs to also include allowable ranges for parameter values. If the list of possible actions (along with allowable parameter ranges) is too long, a shorter list can be created by sampling possible actions and parameter values. To calculate the list of possible actions the simulator has a method calcPossibleActions. The getPossibleActions accessor is then used to obtain the most recently computed list.

If it is not feasible for the simulator to generate any kind of explicit list, there can simply be a method for a controller to test if a given action is possible or not. This approach corresponds to having the controller sample for possible actions instead of the simulator. The advantage of the simulator creating a list of possible actions is that it has a better idea of where best to sample for possible actions. Conversely, a controller probably has a better idea for where to sample for desirable actions. The choice of where to do the sampling therefore depends on the game and the particular implementation.

Often in games there is no method to generate possible actions or even test if a given action is possible. Instead, a controller simply pushes actions it would like to execute onto a stack such that the top of the stack is the most desired action. When it comes time for the simulator to execute an action, it simply keeps popping actions off the stack until it finds one that is possible, at which point it clears the stack and the process repeats. The bottom of the stack is usually some fail-safe action that the controller is sure will always be possible.

2.5.1 Animations and Controllers

Often an action is not possible because its associated animation is incompatible with the currently playing animation. Typically an animation is defined with certain blend points where it can be interrupted and blended into one of some set of alternative animations. If the current animation is not at a blend point, or the blend point is incompatible with the new requested animation, then the given action is not possible. Of course, when deciding if an action is possible the simulator needs to take into account any runtime modifications (such as dropping frames and rescaling) it could employ to make animations compatible.

What if the current animation is not at a compatible blend point (and cannot be modified to make it compatible), but will be in the next couple of frames? Then the action a, associated with the newly requested animation, will not appear in the list of currently possible actions. However, given the choice, a controller might want to pick a, but thinking it is not possible selects some other action b. If the controller had known that a would be available in a few frames it might have waited or chosen some other action c that could execute quickly. If b takes a long time to play its associated animation, then when it is time for the controller to select another action, b's animation could also be at a point incompatible with a. The controller might keep having to select suboptimal actions simply because it is starved of the information it needs to make a proper decision.

A solution could be to define a method that returns a list of soon to be possible actions. Unfortunately, there are likely to be a lot more of these than the list of currently possible actions. Another solution could be to provide a method that returns (approximately in some cases) how many frames (up to some limit) to go before a given action is possible.

To make matters worse, many animations will require the participation of more than one NPC. For example, sports games often require passing the ball from one NPC to another. This requires two different animations to be coordinated with one another and one NPC to end up in the right location and pose to receive the ball. It is therefore easy to see why having controllers simply push actions onto a stack (as described earlier) for the simulator to deal with is so commonplace. For example, if the NPC with the ball wants to pass, the simulator simply needs to find a suitable NPC offering to receive the ball somewhere in their stack of desirable actions.

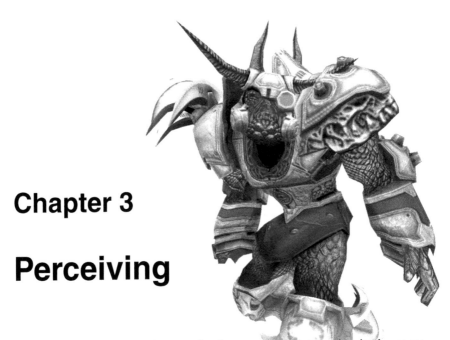

Chapter 3

Perceiving

To act effectively controllers need to know what is happening in the game world. For player characters, the human can be thought of as a central component of the associated controller and the human primarily gets information about the game world through the renderer. For NPCs, access to information about the game world is through simulated perception.

3.1 Renderer

The renderer produces images and sounds that provide the human player with feedback about the game world.[1] Of course, the renderer's sole purpose is not just to provide adequate feedback for control purposes. In particular, stunning graphics and sound are a big part of the enjoyment of a game. High-quality graphics also contribute heavily to the desire to play the game in the first place; although it is often said that the AI and game-play are what keep the player's attention.

Aside from promoting game sales, the visceral and exciting nature of real-time computer graphics has led to widespread interest in the subject which has led to many books. Books on rendering sound are less commonplace, but some sources of information are included in the section on rendering on this book's companion web site.

---

[1]There have been popular games (especially in the early days) that just used textual descriptions to "render" the world. For example, NetHack is a popular text-based game.

From an AI perspective, one of the interesting features of the renderer is how it is used to simulate some of the limitations of real-world perception. For example, just as in reality, players are usually not allowed to see through walls. A fun exception to this rule, used in many games, are weapons with "X-ray" or thermal imaging capabilities.

Some techniques implemented in the renderer are so basic that their role in simulating real-world perception could easily go unnoticed. For example, the use of a perspective projection makes things that are farther away appear smaller when rendered (at least until zooming in with a sniper scope). It is therefore harder to tell an object's identity when it is in the distance. A few more examples of simulated perception that renderers have implemented in various games include heat haze, blurriness of vision after being hit on the head, and even the adjustment of the iris after entering a dark room. You might like to think of some additional examples that you have either seen in games or could imagine being used.

Another important point about the renderer worth mentioning from an AI perspective is its importance for debugging. During debugging it is usually extremely helpful to be able to visually depict an NPC's state of mind, for example, drawing an arrow toward where an NPC thinks the player character is, or drawing a character that an NPC thinks is the biggest danger in a bright color. The ability to somehow visualize an NPC's internal thought processes can often instantly transform a difficult bug into something obvious.

3.1.1   Computer Vision for NPCs

Perception for player characters is handled by the renderer. Therefore, why not use the same renderer to create an image of the world from each NPC's point of view? An NPC's controller could then use the image to figure out the state of the world from its point of view. This would put NPCs and player characters on a level playing field in terms of access to information about the world.

The big disadvantage to using the renderer to implement perception for NPCs is that interpreting an image is hard. Except for additional problems like noisy sensors and calibrating cameras, it is more or less the task that computer vision research tries to solve. In a virtual world various tricks can be used to make the image recognition task easier. For example, an image could be rendered with the enemy in red and everything else in black. Then if there are any red pixels in the resulting image a character can infer that the enemy is visible. Nevertheless, compared to getting information from the game-state directly, computer vision in virtual worlds is still relatively slow and unreliable.[2] In addition, there is the extra cost of rendering extra images: one per NPC, instead of just one per player character.

Even if computer vision worked perfectly, the best it could produce would be a representation of the game world equivalent to the one already in the game-state. It is clearly pointless to go unnecessarily from one representation to another, and then back to the original, especially so if some of the transformations are slow and unreliable.

3.2 Simulated Perception

Instead of rendering an image from an NPC's point of view, an NPC's controller gets information from the world directly from the game-state. However, unless access to the game-state is restricted in some way, NPCs will be able to know too much about the game world. For example, NPCs will be able to see through walls, giving them an unfair advantage over player characters that cannot. In particular, the player character can never hide from NPCs but NPCs can easily hide from the player character. Since hiding can be a fun part of a game, this kind of imbalance can spoil the enjoyment.

To restrict an NPC's access to the game-state, a game will often introduce the idea of a *percept*. A percept is any transformation of information in the game-state, or another percept, into a form suitable for use by an NPC's controller. Not all percepts are used to filter out information, some (as in Section 3.3) just re-express the same information in a more convenient form. Such percepts, that represent values from the game-state without any processing or manipulation, are called *game percepts*. You will recall that Section 2.4.1 in the previous chapter makes an analogous distinction between game actions and higher-level actions.

Section 3.4 describes some higher-level percepts that do filter out information from the game-state. On occasions, percepts can even attempt

---

[2]As pointed out in Section 1.5.2 in Chapter 1, for computer vision research there are many advantages to using virtual worlds.

```
class tgPerception
{
public:
    tgPerception(tgGameState* gs);
    ~tgPerception();
    // Set character from whose point of view percepts are to be calculated
    inline void setMyIndex(int myIndex);
    // Get character from whose point of view percepts are being calculated
    inline int getMyIndex() const;
    // Some example percepts
    inline tgRealVec const& getMyPosition() const;
    inline tgRealVec const& getMyVelocity() const;
    inline tgRealVec const& getTaggedPosition() const;
    inline tgRealVec const& getTaggedVelocity() const;
    tgReal calcMyDistanceToCharacter(int who) const;
    tgReal calcMyDistanceToNearestCharacter() const;
private:
    // Pointer to the game-state object
    tgGameState* gs;
    // Index (from game-state) of "me" character
    int myIndex;
};
```

Listing 3.1. Part of the declaration of the perception class for the tag game.

to reconstruct information that has been filtered out by other percepts (see Section 3.5).

A simple way to implement percepts is as methods of the character's controller class. In general, there will be multiple controllers and each might use a different set of percepts. Inheritance can be used to factor out common percepts into base classes to avoid unnecessary code duplication.

Another possibility is for each controller to have a separate perception object associated with it. The perception object is still conceptually part of the controller, but each controller can then have a different type of perception object; or a different instance of a perception object of the same type; or even (if there is no controller specific state needed) a single shared instance of a perception object. Of course, any combination of these three possibilities can occur across a set of controllers. To avoid duplicating shared percepts, the different perception classes can be arranged in some appropriate inheritance hierarchy.

A big advantage of having a separate perception object is that different perception objects can (potentially) be swapped in and out. For example, there could be one perception object type for when a character is in good health and a subclass for when the character has been hit over the head. The subclass used for concussed controllers could override some methods with versions that deliberately introduce errors into the values returned.

A portion of a simple perception class for a controller in the tag game is shown in Listing 3.1. Some of the methods are defined as virtual so that they can be overridden by subclasses if required. The use of virtual methods incurs a small penalty because inlining virtual methods has no effect. If your game does not need to swap perception objects in and out of controllers, then there is obviously no need to make any of the methods virtual.

Which methods a perception class provides will vary across controllers and games. Nevertheless, there are some common kinds of percepts that recur across games and the remainder of this chapter describes some examples.

3.3   Character-Specific Percepts

One basic type of transformation of information in the game-state is to make it character-specific. This can range from the simple relabeling of pre-existing information, to more complicated calculations such as the computation of relative coordinates.

3.3.1   My Values

At any given instant a controller is selecting actions for a particular NPC. As far as the controller is concerned the NPC in question can be thought of as "me" and it is probably going to make extensive use of various properties associated with "me". It is therefore useful to have a convenient shorthand for these variables. For example, the following definition of the getMyPosition method calculates the position of the NPC that is currently "me":

```
tgRealVec const& tgPerception::getMyPosition() const
{
    return getMyCharacter()->getPosition();
}
```

Similar methods can be written for getMyVelocity, getMyOrientation, getAmITagged, etc. All of these methods just wrap simple accesses to the game-state.

For convenience, the index (from the game-state) of the character that is currently "me" is stored in the class variable myIndex. The value of myIndex is set by the controller prior to deciding which action to pick. That way all the values it requests for "me" will be computed for the correct character. The controller, in turn, knows which character it is picking an action for because it is told by the simulator (see Section 2.4 in Chapter 2).

3.3.2   Other Important Characters

There are often other characters (aside from "me") that are important for a controller. Depending on the game, it could be the "boss monster", or a companion, say, that are important in a controller's decision making. In the tag game, properties of the tagged character (like its position) are likely to figure heavily in the decisions of nontagged characters. For example, the getTaggedPosition method is analogous to the getMyPosition method, but returns the position of the tagged character. Since running away from the tagged character is a central theme of the tag game, there are likely to be many percepts related to the tagged character.

3.3.3   Affordances

Many games add affordances [Gib87] to the environment in the form of labels that are only visible to NPCs. In the context of computer games, an affordance is a piece of information that tells an NPC about actions it can perform at a given location. For example, a doorway might have a label "exit" and a ledge might have a label "jump here". If an NPC decides to leave a room, say, it can access a percept like getPositionNearestExit to look up the nearest "exit" affordance, and then head toward that location.

3.3.4 Relative Values

Relative values, such as relative positions, relative directions, and relative distances, are another common type of percept. For example, the method to calculate the distance of the i th character relative to "me" is calcMyDistanceToCharacter. An example of a slightly more complicated method is calcMyDistanceToNearestCharacter, which is written in terms of calcMyNearestCharacter, which is itself written in terms of calcMyDistanceToCharacter (see Listing 3.2).

Relative values are often combined with percepts related to other named characters. For example, the relative position of the tagged character (to "me") is likely to be an important input to many controllers in the tag game.

Many percepts depend on each other so that calculating one involves calculating its dependents. For example, calcMyDistanceToNearest Character depends on calcMyDistanceToCharacter which in turn depends on calcMyDistanceToCharacter. If some of a percept's dependents have already been calculated, it is wasteful to recompute them. Therefore, percepts should be cached to avoid unnecessary recomputation. If caching is used, care needs to be taken to correctly clear the caches in response to clock ticks, or changing the character from whose point of view percepts are being calculated.

3.4 Partial Observability

If a controller is given full and direct access to the game-state, it has complete access to all the information about the game world and the game world is said to be *fully observable* by the controller. In contrast, if access to the game-state is restricted, then the game world is said to be only *partially observable*. This section introduces some percepts that make the world only partially observable from an NPC controller's perspective.

When the world is only partially observable, then many different game-states are indistinguishable. This is often a good thing as it means controllers can be made more general. That is, many percepts are defined so as to hide unimportant details and emphasize the crucial similarities be-

```
tgCharacter* tgPerception::calcMyNearestCharacter() const
{
    int which = tgGameState::nobody;
    tgReal dMin = Inf;
    for (int i = 0; i < gs->getNumCharacters(); i++)
    {
        if (i == myIndex) { continue; } // Don't include me!

        tgReal d = calcMyDistanceToCharacter(i);
        if (d < dMin)
        {
            dMin = d;
            which = i;
        }
    }
    assert(tgGameState::nobody != which);
    return gs->getCharacter(which);
}

tgReal tgPerception::calcMyDistanceToNearestCharacter() const
{
    tgRealVec p(getMyPosition());
    p.subtract(calcMyNearestCharacter()->getPosition());
    return p.norm();
}
```

Listing 3.2. Definition of percept to calculate the distance to my nearest character.

tween game-states. But as explained earlier, there are occasions when information is deliberately hidden to avoid giving NPCs an unfair advantage. For example, if the tagged character is hidden behind an obstacle, then an NPC is generally not allowed to know its position. From the NPC's point of view, the tagged character could potentially be in any position that is obscured by the obstacle. The set of game-states in which the character is in one of the possible hidden positions it could occupy is referred to as a *belief state*.

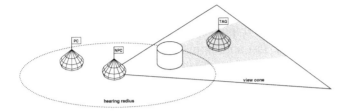

Figure 3.1. Simulated visibility and audibility.

Section 5.3 in Chapter 5 explores how an NPC can maintain its belief state so that it is useful for making decisions. In the meantime, the next few subsections describe some specific ways for simulating some of the limitations of perception that put NPCs and player characters on a more level footing.

3.4.1 Visibility

The image produced by the renderer is often from the direction the player character is looking. Therefore, unless the player character turns her head, she cannot see what is behind her. Many games mitigate this limitation by augmenting the display with an overhead map view. Proper rendering of sound also lets a player hear something sneaking up behind them. Nevertheless, in many games the renderer makes it possible for NPCs to hide from player characters behind opaque objects. To be fair, the converse should also be true: player characters should be able to use objects like walls to hide from NPCs.

For NPCs, instead of using the renderer to implement visibility, a getIsVisible percept can be defined. As the name suggests, the getIsVisible method can be used to determine if a character is visible from another character's point of view. Figure 3.1 shows some simple situations involving visibility in the tag game. In particular, the tagged character is not visible for although it is within the NPC's view cone, it is hidden by an obstacle. In contrast, the player character is outside the view cone, but within the hearing radius and so is visible (or at least audible). See [Leo03] for a good article about building a perception system for a game.

Visibility calculations are commonplace in computer graphics and similar code can be used for calculating visibility percepts. Coherency between frames can allow calculations on previous frames to be reused, which can make a dramatic improvement in the total cost of visibility calculations. In addition, fast approximate visibility tests using bounding boxes and spheres are sometimes sufficient for controllers' purposes. Good references on visibility testing are available from any graphics textbook that describes ray tracing and BSP trees; for example, see [FvDFH95, Shi02].

3.4.2 Simulated Noisy Sensors

The human player will not in general be able to precisely judge object properties like location and speed. Instead, the human will be (implicitly) using values that contain a certain amount of noise. NPCs can be given similar noisy sensor readings by randomly perturbing the true values of various percepts. For example, in the tag game suppose $\mathbf{p} = (x, y)$ is the true position of the tagged character. Then the virtual method getTagged Position could be overridden in a subclass that returns the position $(x + \Delta x, y + \Delta y)$, where Δx and Δy are chosen randomly according to some probability distribution. For example, standard distributions from probability theory can be used, such as a uniform distribution, or a normal distribution with the mean centered on the true position.

3.4.3 Discretization

A percept like getMyDistanceToTagged returns a floating-point number. However, it might be more useful for a controller to predicate its decisions on a more abstract notion of whether the tagged character is close or not. For example, if the distance to the tagged object is d, then the getIsTaggedCloseToMe method computes the predicate: $d < k$, where k is some fixed threshold.

Converting a value (like distance) into a predicate that is either true or false is just one example of *discretization*. In general, a value can be discretized (or bucketed) into more than simply two values. For example, instead of an angle or a unit vector, a direction could be discretized into one of eight compass directions.

Although discretization does hide information about precisely where an object is, it is often done more as a convenience than as a hindrance. For example, in Chapter 6, discretizing positions into a grid is important in order to apply certain types of search algorithms. To show how to define a grid, assume a two-dimensional world bounded by a box with the origin as the lower left hand-corner and (x_{max}, y_{max}) as the upper right-hand corner. Then a grid of $m \times n$ rectangular cells (hexagons or triangles can also be used to tessellate the plane) can be laid over the world, such that the width s and height t of each cell is, respectively, $s = x_{max}/m$ and $t = y_{max}/n$. The grid coordinate (i, j) of a position $\mathbf{p} = (x, y)$ is thus

$$\begin{pmatrix} i \\ j \end{pmatrix} = \begin{pmatrix} \lfloor \frac{x}{s} \rfloor \\ \lfloor \frac{y}{t} \rfloor \end{pmatrix}.$$

3.5 Predictor Percepts

Space Invaders was one of the earliest successful computer games. A key part of the game challenge was being able to accurately anticipate where the invaders would be in the future. This was because the invaders were moving and the bullets took some time to travel. So (unless you got lucky) the bullets would miss if you aimed at the invader's location at the time of firing. Instead, you had to time your shot to end up where the invader would be by the time the bullet arrived. In modern computer games, NPCs sometimes need to use similar kinds of anticipation to shoot back at you. It is convenient therefore to define *predictor percepts* that predict future values. Predictor percepts are also useful for predicting any hidden values. For example, Section 5.3 in Chapter 5 explores how predictor percepts are used to represent a belief state.

In the tag game, a specific example of a predictor percept is calcPosition Tagged Future that predicts the position of the tagged character at some specified time in the future. If the tagged character is currently the player character, then its future position is uncertain because it depends on the future action choices of the human player.

Of course, an NPC can sometimes cheat and know what a player character will do before the appropriate animation is played, but an NPC cannot know for certain (unless the player character is confined somehow) where the player character will be in five minutes. However, if it is important for an NPC to independently show up in the player character's neighborhood in five minutes there are alternatives to trying to predict the location. In particular, if the NPC in question could have plausibly gotten to the

player character's destination in time, then it can just be magically teleported there (or at least moved extra quickly). This will work so long as
the player character does not see the NPC being teleported (unless the ability to teleport is part of the game). It will also appear odd to the player if
an NPC she saw some time ago heading in the opposite direction suddenly
manages to show up later on nearby.

Predicting future values associated with another NPC can be calculated
with more certainty and without resorting to teleporting. This is because
one NPC can, in principle, ask another NPC what it will do in a given
situation. There are, however, reasons why this is not always possible or
desirable:

Influence of the player character. An NPC will react to the player character and so the NPC's future behavior is contingent upon the player
character's future behavior. Since the human player's behavior is
uncertain, then so is the NPC's behavior. Of course, if the player
character is unable to influence an NPC (for example, if it is too far
away), then it may be possible, for a time, to calculate some future
values with certainty.

Random number generators. Random number generators are often used
in games to randomize action choices inside controllers, and other
decisions inside the simulator. Random number generators typically
(unless they have access to specialized hardware) generate pseudorandom numbers. Pseudorandom numbers are not really random
because they are generated by a deterministic computer program,
but they (ideally) share many statistical properties with true random
numbers. If an NPC knew the algorithm by which the pseudorandom
numbers were being generated, it could, in theory, remove the uncertainty they introduce. This would be complicated and (as explained
in the upcoming realistic perception explanation) undesirable.

Game world complexity. Many game world simulators are so complex
that it is hard to accurately approximate their functionality. Conse-
quently, the only certain way of knowing what will happen in the
future is to use the real simulator to look forward in time. In Chapter 6 this is exactly what is described as one way of picking actions.
The problem with going too far into the future is that simulation is

usually CPU-intensive and there is still the problem of predicting what the player character will do.

Approximate simulator. In Chapter 6 an NPC needs to predict both where it and other NPCs will be in the future using a discrete representation of the game world. One way to do this accurately would be to temporarily discard the discrete representation, simulate forward using the continuous representation and the game simulator, and then rediscretize the answer. In practice, this would be slow and cumbersome so the game world's physics are usually also approximated inside the discrete representation directly. To be fast, the approximate game world physics ignores many details but it can still be accurate enough to be useful. Nevertheless the resulting prediction of the NPC's future position is not certain.

Realistic perception. Even if an NPC has access to information that would reduce uncertainty about the game world, it is often undesirable to take advantage of it. A classic example of unrealistic behavior generated from giving a character too much information about the game is given in [Fun99]. In the example, a character uses the simulator to precompute trajectories of falling bricks and then nonchalantly walks through them without any fear of being hit.

Therefore, regardless of whether some future value is really random or not, from the NPC's point of view, it can make sense to think it is. Thus in the tag game, calcPositionTaggedFuture corresponds to the value of a random variable $\mathbf{p}' = (p'_x, p'_y)$ that ranges over possible future positions. Notice that the possible future positions represent a belief state about the future, hence there is a close connection with belief maintenance described in Section 5.3 in Chapter 5.[3]

Before proceeding, you should realize that just because probability is being used to describe predictor percepts, it does not mean that probability

---

[3]In the real world, predictions often have to be made based on noisy sensor readings. In these cases a Kalman filter (see [RN02]) is sometimes used to estimate future (and current) values. In a game world, a similar effect to predicting from noisy sensors can, if required, often be achieved more easily by slightly randomizing the output (as in section 3.4.2) of a simpler prediction method that takes advantage of the availablity of non-noisy sensor values.

has to be used in the implementation of a predictor percept. For example, an implementation of a predictor percept that does not explicitly use probability at all is given toward the end of this section. The implementation falls out as a special case from the more general theoretical framework based on probability. Therefore, regardless of the final implementation, it is still worth exploring the theory behind predictor percepts in a little more detail. To do so, consider just the subproblem of determining the probability that the tagged character's future x-coordinate p'_x, at some fixed time in the future, is in some given interval (a, b). The probability could depend on the current and past values of any number of percepts, but assume the NPC makes the reasonable approximation that it only depends on the current x-position p_x and velocity v_x. Then the NPC needs to calculate the conditional probability $P(a < p'_x < b \mid p_x, v_x)$ that, given the current position and velocity, p'_x will be in the interval (a, b).

Usually the conditional probability distribution is unknown and one possibility is to try and learn it. In particular, learning a conditional probability distribution for the player character can lead to some powerful AI effects. It is, however, complicated and CPU-intensive. In addition, the game designer may not want the NPCs to be too good at predicting the player. As pointed out earlier, even if more accurate or longer term predications are required, it is often easier to cheat. An alternative to learning, or cheating, is to simply define a probability distribution as part of the definition of the behavior of the NPC. That is, the NPC is simply defined to be a character that computes the conditional probability in a certain way. For example, Figure 3.2 defines a possible underlying conditional probability density function from which the conditional probability can be calculated as the area under the curve, as indicated by the shaded region.

However the probability is determined, the final value of the predictor percept needs to be determined for use in a controller. A controller could be defined to take a probability distribution directly as input, but a controller usually expects a single value for the value of a percept. There are numerous ways to generate a single value from a distribution and two of the most common, picking the most likely and picking randomly from the distribution, are described in Appendix A.

In many cases, defining a distribution for a predictor percept at all is overkill. Instead, a percept can just directly compute a single value. You can think of it as a short-circuited version of defining a distribution in terms

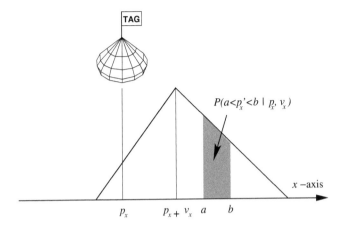

Figure 3.2. Example conditional probability density function.

of the most likely value and then picking the most likely value. As an example, the following code defines the tagged character's future position directly using the current velocity to perform a simple linear extrapolation of the current position:

```
tgRealVec tgPerception::calcTaggedPositionFuture() const
{
    tgRealVec p(getTaggedPosition());
    return p.add(getTaggedVelocity());
}
```

Extrapolating from the current position is also sometimes referred to as *dead reckoning*, and is often used to reduce communication between machines in networked games. The idea is that if two networked instances of a game world use the same dead reckoning algorithm to predict uncertain future values, then communication over the network only has to take place when the difference between the predictions and what subsequently happens exceeds some margin of error.

Note that, predictor percepts that predict the output of a controller blur the distinction between percepts and controllers. For example, if the calcPositionTagged Future is particularly good at predicting the tag character's behavior, then, in theory, its predictions could be used as the controller for the tagged character. Similarily, as mentioned in Section 6.6.1 in Chapter 6, a controller can be used as a predictor percept.

Chapter 4

Reacting

A controller is a function from percepts to actions, and a reactive controller is the special case that has no memory and therefore uses only the current value of the percepts. Because only the current percepts are used, from one call of the calcAction method to the next, a reactive controller (or its associated perception object) is not allowed to store information about the percepts, or action chosen, from the previous invocation. Therefore, if a reactive controller receives identical values for its percepts over and over again, it will select the same action every time, i.e., it is idempotent. Of course, during one invocation of the calcAction method a reactive controller is free to use internal state to store intermediate results. It is just not allowed to use those intermediate results to influence its behavior from one invocation to the next.

Because a reactive controller is idempotent you never have to worry about what state it was left in last time it was used. For example, the same instance of a reactive controller can easily be shared between NPCs. In addition, no state needs to be saved out when the game is turned off or otherwise interrupted. This can result in simpler code and less memory usage. The downside of a reactive controller is that because it is not allowed to remember past situations it can, literally and figuratively, end up going around in circles. Nevertheless, reactive controllers are useful, versatile, and powerful. For example, some insects appear to use primarily reactive controllers and there are some classic publications in the AI literature that used computer games to argue for reactive systems as a basis for AI [AC87, Cha91].

4.1 Definition of a Reactive Controller

A reactive controller (or policy) is a function ϕ from percepts $\mathbf{x} = (x_0, \ldots, x_{m-1})$ to actions $a(\mathbf{y})$ such that

$$\phi(\mathbf{x}) = a(\mathbf{y}), \tag{4.1}$$

where x_i is the current value[1] of percept i and $\mathbf{y} = (y_0, \ldots, y_{k-1})$ are the k action parameters. Note that, in general, $\mathbf{x}$ represents a belief state as described in Section 3.4 in Chapter 3.

In the tag game there is only one game action, the move action. But it takes two parameters that indicate the direction to move, and it is the controller's job to determine them. More realistic games will require the controller to choose from many possible actions, some or all of which may have parameters. If some of the actions do have parameters, then selecting an action is a two-step process: step one is to select the action and step two is, given the selected action, to choose desirable parameters. If desirable parameters cannot be found, then step one needs to be repeated until a different action is selected for which suitable parameters can be found.

Providing a definition of a reactive controller does not answer the more interesting question: where do controllers come from? The answer is that they are either defined by the game developer, or learned. The focus of Chapter 7 is on the topic of learning controllers, while this and the next two chapters concentrate on defining them directly.

4.1.1 Stochastic Version of a Reactive Controller

Ignoring the problem of picking parameters for now, assume that the controller's sole task is to pick one of n possible actions: $a_0, \ldots, a_{n-1}$. The stochastic version of a reactive controller does not pick an action directly. Instead, it defines a conditional probability distribution over the possible

---

[1]The "value" of a percept need not be a numerical value, it can be a Boolean value (true or false), a label, a set of label, a string, a set of strings, etc.

actions and uses one of the methods described in Appendix A to pick an action. The conditional distribution $P(a_i|\mathbf{x})$ specifies the probability of picking each a_i, given the current values of the percepts.

An interesting special case is when, regardless of the value of the percepts $\mathbf{x}$, the probability $1/n$ is unconditionally assigned to each action (i.e., the probability distribution is the uniform distribution). Then picking randomly from the distribution gives an equal chance of selecting any of the actions. The resulting controller is called the *random controller* and is useful for stress-testing a game.

In general, the probability assigned to each action should represent the probability that it is the action you want the NPC to pick in the current situation. For example, if an NPC is far away from a dangerous enemy, then perhaps it is better for the NPC to run away, but you'd also be happy if it stays where it is for a while. Then you would assign a 70% chance, say, to the run-away action, and a 30% chance to the stay action. If you are sure which action you want the NPC to do in every situation, then there is obviously no need to use a stochastic controller.

Note that, since a stochastic reactive controller is still reactive, if it receives identical values for its percepts over and over again, it will select the same probability distribution every time. Although, if one of the methods used in Appendix A is then used to pick an action randomly from the distribtion, then the final action that gets sent to the simulator will of course vary.[2]

As for a deterministic controller, picking parameters in a stochastic controller can be done as a separate step. For example, suppose an action a has been chosen and that it can take one of k parameter values: $y_0, \ldots, y_{k-1}$. Then another conditional probability distribution $P(y_i|a, \mathbf{x})$ gives the probability of picking y_i, given the action choice a and the current value of the percepts.

If the parameter is continuous, then there is some underlying conditional probability density function. If there is more than one parameter and they are not independent, or cannot be treated (as an approximation) as if they are independent, then the situation gets complicated and is beyond

---

[2]To avoid violating the definition of a reactive controller as idempotent, the seed to the random number generator must be included in the percepts, in which case identical percepts will yield an identical action choice. Alternatively, the picking randomly part can be considered as a separate process.

the scope of this book. Similarly, complications arise if picking actions and parameters cannot be done independently.

Now that you know what a stochastic controller is, it is worth quickly pointing out why you might want to use one:

- it is often more exciting to play against NPCs who are not completely predictable.

- as pointed out in Section 3.4.2 and Section 3.5 in the previous chapter, the inputs to a controller can contain uncertainty, so it makes sense that the outputs can, too. That is, it is hard to know in advance precisely what the best action is, so randomizing allows the AI programmer to hedge.

- randomness can break symmetries to avoid, for example, an NPC getting stuck in a corner forever.

- in the real world actuators (like sensors) can be noisy. For example, holding an object completely still is difficult and the object usually wobbles slightly. In games where there is a sniper mode this wobbling is sometimes modeled for the player character by randomly moving the displayed image around in the sniper mode. For NPCs a similar effect can be achieved by slightly randomizing the output of its aiming controller.

- from the NPC's point of view, the player character is somewhat enigmatic. Even if an NPC tries to learn to predict the player character's actions, there will be hidden variables that (given the available percepts) make aspects of the player's behavior impenetrable. For example, the player might behave differently when she is hungry, but there is no realistic way to define a percept to say how hungry the player is. For the purposes of learning, the hidden variables can be modeled as random variables whose distribution must be determined from the data. A crude way to make the NPC's behavior also appear (to the player) somewhat enigmatic is, therefore, to add randomness to the NPC's controller output.

- humans often see patterns in, and ascribe meaning to, random events. Somewhat like seeing patterns in the clouds, players often mistake blind luck for intelligence. This can obviously work both ways and NPCs could end up looking stupid by not picking the most obvious action.

4.2 Simple Functions of Percepts

Even relatively uncomplicated functions from percepts to actions can yield interesting behavior. For example, the controller in Listing 4.1 causes a character to pursue the nearest character if it is tagged, and run away otherwise.

```
void tgControllerNPC::calcAction(int whoami)
{
    perception->setMyIndex( whoami );
    tgRealVec v( perception->getMyPosition() );

    if ( perception->getAmITagged() )
    { // Pursuit
        v.subtract( perception->getMyNearestCharacterPosition() );
        v.scale( -1.0 ); // run towards
    }
    else
    { // Evasion
        v.subtract( perception->getTaggedPosition() );
    }
    v.normalize();
    v.scale( perception->getMyMaxSpeed() );
    v.subtract( perception->getMyVelocity() );
    action.setDesiredVelocity( v );
}
```

Listing 4.1. Simple pursuit and evasion controller for the tag game.

Pursuit and evasion are two examples of *steering behaviors*. A more complex example of a steering behavior is the *boids* model of flocks, herds, and schools. The boids model was first published in [Rey87], and since then it has been widely used in games and movies. Boids flocking behavior is obtained by adding together three weighted steering components *alignment* $\mathbf{v}_a$, *cohesion* $\mathbf{v}_c$, and *separation* $\mathbf{v}_s$ to obtain the overall desired velocity $\mathbf{v}_d$.

$$\mathbf{v}_d = w_0 \hat{\mathbf{v}}_a + w_1 \hat{\mathbf{v}}_c + w_2 \hat{\mathbf{v}}_s$$

Different relative weights w_0, w_1 and w_2 give rise to different kind of flocks. For example, a lower weight for cohesion gives rise to a more loosely knit flock. Note that, if the weights sum to one, then $\mathbf{v}_d$ will be automatically normalized.

The individual steering components are all computed with respect to nearby characters. A percept calcCharactersNearMe is therefore used to compute the list of characters within some threshold. The threshold itself is another one of the boid flocking model parameters.

The alignment steering component $\mathbf{v}_a$ is the average orientation of the nearby characters. Similarly, cohesion $\mathbf{v}_c$ is a vector that points toward the nearby characters' average position. Separation is slightly more complicated. Intuitively, if there were only two characters, the separation component would be a vector pointing in the opposite direction to the other character. With multiple characters nearby, separation is defined as the sum of all the normalized vectors pointing away from each character, scaled by the inverse of the distance:

$$\mathbf{v}_s = \sum_i \frac{\hat{\mathbf{q}}_i}{|\mathbf{q}_i|},$$

where $\mathbf{q}_i = \mathbf{p}_i - \mathbf{p}$, $\mathbf{p}$ is "my" position and $\mathbf{p}_i$ is the position of nearby character i.

Obviously, because each flock member is in a slightly different situation, the steering vector $\mathbf{v}_d$ needs to be computed separately for each individual. But since flocking can be implemented as an idempotent reactive controller, the same identical instance of the controller can be used for an entire flock.

A good source of further details on the boid flocking model, its variations, and a wide range of additional steering behaviors is [Rey99]. There is also an open source library called OpenSteer that implements a wide variety of important steering behaviors (see this book's companion web site for a pointer to the code).

```
void tgControllerNPC::calcAction(int myIndex)
{
    perception->setMyIndex(myIndex);

    tgObstacle* obj = perception->calcMyNearestObstacle();
    if ( perception->calcAmICollidingSoonWith(obj) )
    {
        avoidCollision(obj);
    }
    else
    {
        flock();
    }
}
```

Listing 4.2. Controller that gives priority to avoiding collisions.

4.3   Reactive Production Rules

One common steering behavior is collision avoidance. Avoiding collisions is usually a high priority, higher than maintaining a flock forma-
tion, for example. It is convenient therefore to be able to write conditional rules to express the different priorities. For example, suppose the
tgControllerNPC class has methods avoidCollision and flock that, respectively, produce steering vectors to avoid collisions and maintain the boid
flocking model. In addition, suppose there is a percept calcIsCollsionsIm-
mininent, then Listing 4.2 shows a conditional controller that gives priority
to avoiding collisions.

In general, conditional rules have the form of *if-then* rules and are referred to as *production rules*.[3] The *if* part contains a test, or firing condi-
tion, and the *then* part executes some action or subcontroller. When the test
is true the rule is said to have fired or activated. Production rules can be
nested and arranged in hierarchies to create elaborate behaviors. Production rules are also important for implementing more general, nonreactive,
controllers as explained in Section 5.4.3 of the next chapter.

---

[3]Production rule systems consist only of pattern matching rules, rather than procedural
code as in Listing 4.2.

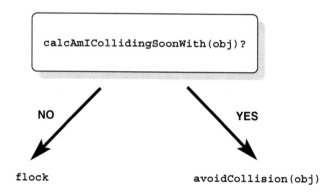

Figure 4.1. Example of a decision stump.

4.4   Decision Trees

Figure 4.1 shows the same conditional rule as in Listing 4.2, but represented as a decision tree. More specifically, it is a tree with only one internal node, which is commonly referred to as a *decision stump*. In general, a decision tree consists of a number of nodes and branches. The leaf nodes represent decisions, i.e. action choices. The internal (nonleaf) nodes represent tests and each node has as many branches as there are possible answers to the test. A controller uses a decision tree to pick an action by evaluating tests and taking the branch that corresponds to the result. When the controller gets to a leaf, then that is the action to choose. For example, Figure 4.2 shows a decision tree that might be used by a high-level controller in the tag game. The controller is not meant to be taken seriously as a legitimate controller, but there are a couple of things to note:

- not all tests in a decision tree have to be binary. For example, in the diagram the percept calcDistanceToTagged returns a Boolean. In general, a test can also return an integer or even a float. If a test does return a number over a wide possible range, then usually each branch represents a bucket of values.

- not all the leaf nodes have to be game actions. For example, in the figure only one leaf node sets the desired velocity. The others call other methods of the controller class, which implement subcontrollers, and may be decision trees themselves.

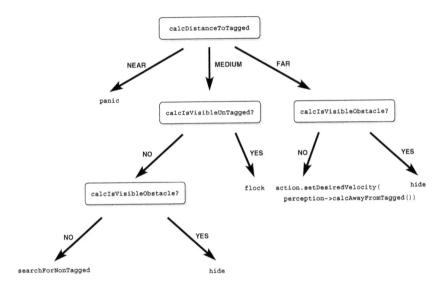

Figure 4.2. Example of a decision tree.

- the same test in a different part of the tree can yield different action choices. For example, in the figure an NPC that is far from the tagged character will run even farther away if it cannot see an obstacle to hide behind. But an NPC that is only a medium distance to the tagged character, and cannot see another untagged character, will search for a fellow untagged character.

Decision trees are easy to program (see this book's companion web site for pointers) and have been used as a representation for controllers in computer games. One important reason they are suitable representation is that, with a suitable Graphical User Interface (GUI), they can be created and maintained by nonprogrammers.

Decision trees are closely related to production rules in that a decision tree can easily be converted into a set of rules. In particular, there is a rule for each leaf such that the *if*-part is the conjunction of each of the tests on the way from the root to the leaf; and the *then*-part is just the action at the leaf node.

Trees and production rules are also both popular representations for the output of machine learning algorithms. CART and C4.5 are two classic machine learning programs that can output decision trees or production rules (see [HTF01]). More recent machine learning algorithms use weighted forests of decision trees (or stumps) and new decision tree-like data structures like AD-trees. The big advantage decision trees and production rules have as a representation of a learned function is that, unlike neural network weights for instance, they can be inspected to see if they make sense intuitively (see [WF99]).

4.4.1 Stochastic Decision Trees

If instead of a single action choice at each leaf node there is a probability distribution defined over all possible actions, then a decision tree can be used to represent a stochastic controller. The deterministic version of a decision tree can be thought of as the special case of a stochastic one in which all the probability is assigned to a single action. Specifying probabilities for all the possible actions is obviously more work. When selecting continuous parameter values, the leaf node will typically specify *sufficient statistics* that completely specify some standard distribution. For example, a leaf node could specify the mean and standard deviation that is then used to define a normal distribution.

Note that, in the stochastic version of a decision tree, there is no randomness in selecting a probability distribution at a leaf node. That is, given the current values of the percepts the leaf node is selected deterministically using the tests at the internal nodes. The stochastic nature of the controller is in the fact that it outputs a probability distribution instead of a single action. As described earlier, one of the methods described in Appendix A can then be used to (if desired) add randomness when picking an action according to the distribution.

If, as is usually the case, an NPC can choose a new action every few frames, then you have to be careful when picking randomly from a distribution to not get an NPC that flip-flops between decisions. For example, an NPC might randomly pick a different action each time and never get far executing either one. The effect the human sees on the screen in such cases is often of an NPC having a violent twitching fit! The solution is to make the controller take into account previous action choices, but that would require remembering, which is covered in the next chapter. The reason twitching is not such a concern with a deterministic controller (although it can happen at decision boundaries) is because, in a similar situation, the controller is likely to choose a similar action.

4.5   Logical Inference

An *if-then* rule, like those in Section 4.3, is an example of a simple inference rule. In academic AI many other more sophisticated types of inference rules have been studied, and it is conceivable that these other inference rules could be used in games to pick actions. One particularly important set of inference rules is known as first-order logic. First-order logic
was created as a formal language for mathematics, but it is sufficiently expressive that it has been widely used in AI for representing various problem
domains.

Here is an example of an inference rule that could be used by a controller:

$$\forall x \; P(x) \Rightarrow Q(x), \; P(a) \vdash Q(a).$$

What it says is that if every x that is a P is also a Q, and a is a P, then
a must also be Q. P and Q can be any predicates (i.e., Boolean valued
functions) so if x can range over all NPCs in a game, $P(x)$ represents "x
is a plumber", $Q(x)$ represents "x has a mustache", and a is Mario, then
the inference rule allows the controller to infer that Mario has a mustache.
This could be useful if an NPC had the task of choosing a gift for his
friend Mario the plumber, but was never explicitly told that Mario had a
mustache. Note that, with the same interpretation of P and Q, the rule does
not allow the controller to infer that an NPC is a plumber just because he
has a mustache.

Aside from its expressive power, the big advantage of using first-order
logic is that it has a proof system with some reassuring properties:

Sound. The proof system is sound. This means that if you start out with a
set of assumptions, then any sentence that you prove is (with respect
to the initial assumptions) true. Note that, this says nothing about
whether the initial assumptions are true, and indeed if they contain
a contradiction, then you will be able to prove anything!

Complete. The proof system is complete, i.e., any true sentence can be
proved.

Importantly for computer games, the proof system for first-order logic
can be embodied in a computer program known as a *theorem prover*. Prolog is a well-known example of a programming language that contains a

built-in theorem prover [Lin98, RN02]. Using a theorem prover inside a controller is therefore potentially powerful, as an NPC could infer all sorts of consequences of what it knows and appear highly intelligent. Unfortunately, using a theorem prover in games faces a number of obstacles:

1. if a sentence is true, it can potentially take an exponential amount of time for the theorem prover to prove it. Researchers have proposed more restricted proof systems for first-order logic that are sound, but not complete. The advantage of these limited systems is that they are guaranteed to succeed in polynomial time if the sentence is true.

2. first-order logic is only *semidecidable*. This means that if a sentence is false, the theorem prover might never be able to prove it. That is, the theorem prover might go into an infinite loop, but there is no way to tell (in general) that it has gone into an infinite loop, or that it is just about to return the answer. This makes it difficult to know when the theorem prover should be set to time out.

3. theorem provers potentially use an enormous amounts of memory.

4. in general, to prove anything useful, a character needs a lot of commonsense knowledge. The Cyc project is attempting to alleviate this problem by creating a vast KB of commonsense knowledge [Len95].

5. theorem provers typically do not have much support for representing uncertainty. There have been attempts to combine first-order logic and probability theory, but the work is presently largely of theoretical interest.

Because of the obstacles to using first-order logic in games, a more reasonable alternative is to use propositional logic. Propositional logic is a subset of first-order logic that does not include any variables. Propositional logic is fully decidable, but testing the validity of a proposition can still take an exponential amount of time in the worst case. However, there are sound but incomplete "SAT" solvers that use stochastic methods to quickly solve many nontrivial problems [KS03].

One downside of propositional logic is that because it does not have variables, to express the fact that all NPCs in the game are green, say, you cannot write $\forall x \; Green(x)$. Instead, you have to write out a separate proposition for each NPC. For example, if there are three NPCs called Fred, Mary, and Bill, you'd have to write out

$$FredGreen \land MaryGreen \land BillGreen.$$

If there are a lot of NPCs this can get tiresome, and if there are a lot of properties each NPC can possess, then there are an exponential number of potential propositions. There are tools for automatically converting first-order logic style expressions to propositions, but the end result can still consume a lot of memory.

Aside from any technical difficulties, logical reasoning would require a game design that justified its inclusion, for example, if the game needed to simulate human logical reasoning, or if the game world was a complex domain that required runtime logical inference. The behavior rules that game developers normally write can be thought of as the result of their own logical inference. That is, they think in advance about which rules an NPC needs to operate effectively in their world, given the game physics and the NPC's capabilities.

Chapter 5

Remembering

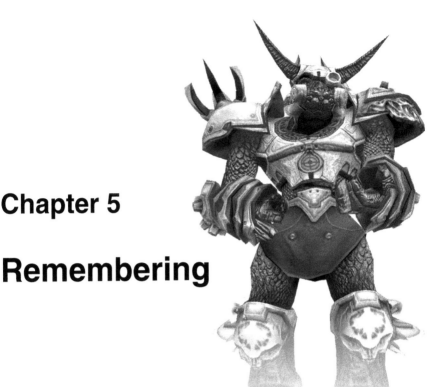

Because reactive controllers are idempotent they are simple to use, but they also have serious drawbacks. For example, because a reactive controller cannot remember previous percepts and actions, it cannot remember which action it picked last time it was in the same situation. When it finds itself in the same situation as before, it cannot therefore decide to pick a different action from before. If last time the choice turned out to be a bad one, then a reactive controller will carry on making the same mistake over and over again, just like a fly repeatedly hitting a window pane. Since there is no way for it to distinguish seeing a situation once to seeing it a thousand times, it cannot even count how many times it has been in the same situation before.

Coupled with a way to randomly pick from the resulting distribution, a stochastic reactive controller can output different actions in the same situation. But this does not fundamentally alter the limitations of a reactive controller because, on average, the frequency with which it picks different actions will, in identical situations, be the same.[1]

---

[1]If the percepts include a value that is always different (like the current time), then no two situations are ever the same. If no two situations are the same, then obviously the problem of not being able to recognize being in the same situation never arises. But normally percepts are chosen so as to emphasize the similarity between game-states, as this makes controllers more general.

The only way to address the inherent limitations of a reactive controller is to permit the controller, and associated perception object, to remember the past values of percepts. Such controllers have no inherent limitations and can be programmed to compute any computable function from percepts to actions.

5.1 Definition of a Controller

Except that it can use previous values of percepts, the definition of a controller is similar to the definition of a reactive controller given in Equation 4.1 in the previous chapter. In particular, if the percepts at time t are denoted $\mathbf{x}^t = (x_0^t, \ldots, x_{m-1}^t)$, then a controller ϕ is a function from percepts to actions such that

$$\phi(\mathbf{x}^0, \ldots, \mathbf{x}^t) = a(\mathbf{y}), \qquad (5.1)$$

where $\mathbf{y}$ are the action parameters.

For the case where there are no parameters and the sole task is to pick one of n actions, $a_0, \ldots, a_{n-1}$, the stochastic version of a controller is defined by a conditional probability distribution over the possible actions. Similar to the definition in 4.1.1 in the last chapter, the conditional probability distribution $P(a_i | \mathbf{x}^0, \ldots, \mathbf{x}^t)$ specifies the probability of picking each a_i, given the values of the percepts. Once again, one of the methods described in Appendix A can be used to pick a single action from the distribution.

5.2 Memory Percepts

Equation 5.1 expresses a controller's ability to use any of the past percepts in its calculations. That does not mean a controller has to use all the past percepts, and in practice a controller would quickly run out of memory if it had to remember the value of every single percept it has ever seen. Instead, a controller remembers certain key percepts, like the last place it saw the tagged character, or summary percepts, like the number of times it has been chased around a particular obstacle. These percepts are called *memory percepts*.

Note that although the state used to store memory percepts is typically part of the perception object, any controller that makes use of a memory percept is automatically stateful, and no longer reactive. That is because the function the controller is computing can depend on some previous percepts' values, and not just on the current ones. Depending on what those previous values are, the controller can thus behave differently in two otherwise identical situations. Conceptually, where the state used to remember the previous percepts' values happens to be located is an irrelevant detail. However, from an implementation perspective, it does keep the code simpler if the state can all be added in the perception object, but as explained in Section 5.4 this is not always desirable. The advantage to keeping the state in the perception object is that NPCs can share a controller instance. The perception object is then responsible for managing the state associated with each character. This can be done by having a separate perception object instance for each character, but a simpler alternative is used in what follows.

Memory percepts are often stored on a per character basis, but information can also be remembered on a per level basis, or a per location basis, etc. As an example of a memory percept, consider getWhoLastTaggedMe that remembers which character was the last one who tagged "me". This information might be useful to a controller for an NPC that likes to get revenge. Remember that which character is "me" is indicated by the myIndex class variable and changes according to whose turn it is to select an action.

Because the information is not needed by the simulator, the game-state does not store information about who last tagged who and the getWhoLast TaggedMe method cannot therefore be a function of the game-state. Of course, it is possible to imagine a version of the tag game where it is important for the simulator to record who last tagged who, for example, if a rule was added that prevented a character tagging back the character who just tagged them. But even then the game-state would only need to store the information for the currently tagged character. The point is that as the game stands, the information is not needed by the simulator and is therefore not (and should not be) stored in the game-state.

Since the game-state does not know which character last tagged "me", the information needs to be stored in the perception object. There are a variety of ways to do this, but a simple solution is to add a new private class variable to the perception object (or a subclass): lastTaggedByList. The lastTaggedbyList is a list (e.g., an array) with an entry for each character, such that the i th entry is the index of the last character who tagged character *i*. The percept getWhoLastTaggedMe then simply looks up the corresponding entry in lastTaggedByList:

```
int tgPerception::getWhoLastTaggedMe() const
{
    return lastTaggedByList[myIndex];
}
```

For the getWhoLastTaggedMe method to return the correct answer lastTagged ByList had better be kept up-to-date, and this is where adding state to controllers gets tricky. The problem is that, unless the simulator polls every controller every time the game-state changes, events can happen in the game world without the controllers ever becoming aware of them. To illustrate the problem, suppose the perception object has a method updateLastTagged that checks if the tagged character changed since it was last called and updates the lastTagged variable accordingly:

```
void tgPerception::updateLastTagged()
{
    int const taggedIndex = getTaggedIndex();
    // Note: lastTaggedIndex is a class varaible
    if ( taggedIndex != lastTaggedIndex )
    { // A new character has been tagged since last update
        // Assume lastTaggedIndex tagged taggedIndex
        lastTaggedByList[ taggedIndex ] = lastTaggedIndex;
        lastTaggedIndex = taggedIndex;
    }
}
```

The potential problem is with the assumption that the character with index lastTaggedIndex was the one who tagged the character with index taggedIndex. For example, suppose character *i* was tagged by character *j* who then tagged character *k* all before the updateLastTagged was called. This might happen if time-slicing meant that controllers were not always invoked and the tag events were just a consequence of collisions handled by the simulator. When a controller was finally called and the perception object updated, the lastTaggedByList would be updated with the wrong information! In particular, it would incorrectly assert that character k was tagged directly by character i. Character i might then unfairly receive the wrath of character k that should have been directed at character j. To the human watching all this take place, character k's behavior would seem puzzling indeed. Obviously this example is somewhat contrived but the problem is a genuine one.

There are a number of solutions to the problem. For example, an event-based message passing system could be used, such that if a tagging event occurs, then an appropriate update message gets sent. Alternatively, all perception objects could share a common instance of another perception object that contains all the state information. The common instance has an update method that needs to be called whenever the game-state changes, that way there is no danger of missing important events. Having to call the update method so often can cause difficulties if the CPU budget is tight. Depending on the game and if you are willing to tolerate the odd mistake, it may therefore be possible to call it less often. However, once the controller's state is allowed to get out-of-date, bugs that are difficult to track down can crop up unexpectedly.

5.2.1 Using Memory Percepts

Memory percepts can be used to make an NPC's behavior depend on what has happened in the past. For example, in role-playing games NPCs typically choose what to say based on what the player character has already achieved.

Fortunately, the mechanics of using memory percepts is trivial. In particular, they can be used wherever regular percepts are used. For example, looking back at the previous chapter, memory percepts can be used in controllers that are simple functions of percepts (see Section 4.2), production rules (see Section 4.3 and also Section 5.4.3 later on in this chapter), and decision trees (see Section 4.4).

Listing 5.1 shows a possible method of a controller class in the tag game that uses the getWhoLastTaggedMe memory percept to determine who the tagged character should chase. The calcWhoToChase method will be called from the calcAction method whenever the tagged character (assuming it is not currently also the player character) needs to compute an action.

```
tgCharacter* tgControllerNPC::calcWhoToChase()
{
    tgCharacter* const c = perception->calcMyNearestCharacter();
    tgCharacter* const t = perception->getTaggedCharacter();

    // Sometimes it is obvious who to chase
    if (c == t) { return c; }

    tgReal const dc = perception->calcMyDistanceToNearestCharacter();
    // If a character is really close, chase them no matter what
    // Note: minChaseDist is part of the character definition passed in
    // to the controller's constructor
    if (dc < minChaseDist) { return c; }

    tgReal const dt = perception->calcMyDistanceToTaggedCharacter();
    // If the character who last tagged me is a lot farther away forget it
    // Note: minChaseRatio is also part of the character definition
    if (dt/dc < minChaseRatio) { return c; }

    // OK, it's reasonable to chase the character who last tagged me
    return t;
}
```

Listing 5.1. Decide who to chase.

5.3 Belief Maintenance

Recall from Section 3.4 in Chapter 3 that a belief state is the set of possible game-states that is consistent with the current percept values. So, for example, if the tagged character is not visible it could potentially be in any obscured location. Based on the values of its memory percepts, an NPC could attempt to predict where the tagged character is. The simplest prediction an NPC can make is to predict that the tagged character is exactly where it last saw it.

Figure 5.1 illustrates an example of a common problem that arises with predicting that hidden state remains unchanged. On the left is the situation

Figure 5.1. An NPC's beliefs can become out-of-date.

when an NPC last saw the tagged character. Later on, the NPC has turned away and the tagged character has sneaked up behind it. But on the right the NPC foolishly believes the tagged character is still where it was. The problem is that the memory percept taggedLastKnownPosition is no longer an accurate representation of the game-state. But the NPC is still using it to predict that the unseen portions of the game world have not changed. If the NPC picks actions based on incorrect beliefs it will make bad choices. It is therefore important for an NPC to try and realize when its beliefs are unreliable and, if possible, to maintain them in a useful state. This is called belief (or truth) maintenance.

5.3.1 Invalidating Memory Percepts

Typically, the longer it was since the memory percept was refreshed, the more unreliable it is. A simple mechanism to model this is to represent the memory percept as an interval (see [Fun99]). When the memory percept is refreshed the interval is of width zero, then widens over time. If at any point an NPC wants to use the memory percept to make a prediction about the current game-state, it checks how wide it has become. If the width is above some acceptable threshold, then it is either not used, or if the value is important, an *information gathering* action is selected.

As the name suggests, an information gathering action is one whose purpose is to gather information. The player character also often chooses information gathering actions, for example, by running out to look where an enemy is. Many games include a stealth mode in which there are special information gathering actions such as "lean" that allow the player character to peek around corners without being seen.

Uniformly widening the interval representing a memory percept is simple and effective, but there are also more sophisticated approaches. For example, the interval could be widened more in some directions than others. In the case of the taggedLastKnownPosn percept, it could be widened more in the direction the tagged character was last seen to be traveling.

A still more sophisticated approach is to represent a memory percept as a probability distribution, similar to the approach described in Section 3.5 in Chapter 3. For example, for taggedLastKnownPosn the distribution represents the probability of the tagged character being in a certain area of the map. When the memory percept is refreshed all the probability is on the region where the tagged character is perceived to be. The entropy of the probability distribution then gradually increases over time, possibly at different rates in different directions. So long as the tagged character is not visible, the probability it is in a visible area needs to be (assuming there are no cloaking devices in the game) set to zero. These ideas are explored more fully in [IB02]. More recently, in [Ber04], a related and popular AI technique called *particle filtering* is applied to games. See [RN02] for more on sophisticated probabilistic reasoning in the context of general AI. Also see Section 6.6 in Chapter 6 for some additional ideas on how NPCs can model adversaries.

The full power of being able to predict the current game-state from past information is illustrated by the prowess of the well-known cyberathlete Thresh. When Thresh played Doom or Quake he used a tactic that whenever he saw a player enter a room with a single exit he would not follow them inside. Instead, he would wait patiently outside to ambush them when they came out. If he remembered the contents of the room, he would even simulate them in his mind's eye going to pick up the rocket launcher, say, and then heading out. He was so precise that on occasions he could time firing a rocket at the entrance so that the rocket exploded just as the player emerged.

It is possible that players would assume NPCs with the same ability to predict hidden state as well as Thresh were cheating! Such NPCs might also not be much fun for some players, especially beginners, to play against (which is something to bear in mind before expending a lot of effort on an NPC's belief maintenance abilites).

5.3.2 Cheating

If an NPC really needs to know the location of a character obscured from view, then it can just cheat by looking it up in the game-state.[2] The downside of this kind of cheating is that human players can often tell. This can be frustrating and contribute to making playing against NPCs less fun than playing against other humans over a network. But by using simulated noisy sensors (see Section 3.4.2 in Chapter 3) to look up values in the game-state, humans players can often be fooled for much longer as to whether the NPCs are cheating or just being smart. This is because the noisy sensors will only return the correct (or near correct) answer some of the time.

Cheating can also be used in a more subtle way to check on the validity of memory percepts. In particular, by checking the degree of divergence between a memory percept and the corresponding value in the game-state, an NPC can realize when a memory percept is stale. If necessary it can then generate an information gathering action to discover the new value by legitimate means. Within reason, it is unlikely a player could quickly spot this kind of cheating, especially if randomness was introduced, for example, the NPC could be forced to use a noisy sensor to look up the true value of a memory percept. That way it would sometimes make the wrong decision about whether or not it needed to do any information gathering. To the player, this should look like highly realistic behavior.

NPCs can also use the ability to cheat to help player characters. For example, an NPC in a game might be able to throw hand grenades that damage all players within some blast radius. If the NPC's controller does not know where the player is (for example, the player character is hiding behind a rock), it might randomly throw a grenade nearby the player character. If the player character and NPC are supposed to be enemies, then, on the face of it, damaging the player character seems desirable. The "real" goal of the NPC is, however, to make the game fun. The game designer might therefore have mandated that the probability of throwing a grenade that will damage the player character should go down if the player character is nearly dead. That way the player might enjoy the game more as she survives long enough to get to the next health pack while grenades

---

[2]Note that, when predictor percepts are predicting future vales, this kind of cheating is obviously not possible because the future game-state does not yet exist.

"luckily" explode off in the distance. Sometimes such "cheating" (even with good intentions) can backfire and the feeling of danger is spoiled, but game designers need the option of making such choices.

5.4 Mental State Variables

The calcWhoToChase method in Listing 5.1 will decide to chase the character who last tagged "me", unless it is too far away relative to the nearest character. On successive calls to the calcWhoToChase method it is quite possible that a different character will be chosen to chase. This would happen, for example, if the tagged character was chasing the one who last tagged it and a different character wandered too close. In that case, the tagged character would break off the current chase and begin chasing the nearest character. If the nearest character got far enough away, it would return to chasing the character who last tagged it. There is nothing wrong with this behavior and given the continuous nature of movement in the tag game it would all look smooth and natural. But suppose that (for the sake of argument) once the tagged character has started chasing a character, the game developer wants to make it exhibit more goal commitment and continue chasing that character no matter what.

If there was a memory percept like getWhoLastChasing, then changing the controller as desired would be easy. To implement getWhoLastChasing there would have to be a list that stored, for each character, who it last chased. But how could the information about who a character is currently chasing be calculated from the game-state? It could not. You can imagine writing code to make a reasonable guess at who is being chased, but if there are two characters nearby (or even roughly in the same direction from the tagged character) it would be hard to be certain. The reason is that the notion of chasing a character really relates to a character's internal mental state. Such quantities are referred to as *mental state variables*.

The same reasons it is inappropriate to store memory percepts in the game-state, mentioned earlier in Section 5.2, also apply to mental state variables. Mental state variables could be stored as memory percepts, but unlike other percepts they are not just functions of the game-state or other percepts. In particular, they are also functions of a controller's internal state. Thus if they were memory percepts, then they would be part of the output of a controller, which breaks the rule that controllers only output actions. As with all good programming practice, there is nothing to stop you breaking the rules but it is likely to quickly lead to confusing and hard-to-maintain code. It therefore reinforces their internal hidden nature if mental state variables are represented as private member variables within the controller class. In the tag game, that means in the tgController class or one of its subclasses. Explicitly adding state to the controller class means that there has to a be a separate controller instance for each character.

Like the state in the perception objects, the state in controllers needs to be kept up-to-date. However, it is not quite so important for controllers because the mental states are not simple functions of the game-state and it is therefore harder for an outside observer (like the player) to say for sure that a character is behaving wrongly. That is, if you are lucky, unusual behavior might be attributed to an NPC's personality. However, you should obviously not rely on being afforded such a kind interpretation of your bugs.

5.4.1 Emotions

NPC's emotions act as a sort of rough summary of past events. This makes sense if you think for a moment about the real world. For example, if a sequence of bad events happens to you, you might well end up feeling angry without necessarily being able to recall all the specific events that made you so. The same would apply to feeling happy, or bored, etc. This is not the place to get into a philosophical debate about the true nature of emotions (see [Wri97] if you are interested). But having mental state variables like angerLevel, isHappy, etc. is common, useful, and powerful.

For example, every time an NPC is tagged its anger level could go up and then slowly subside over time when it was not tagged. If it got tagged when it was really angry it would feverishly chase the character who tagged it, otherwise it would go for the nearest character. The anger level toward each individual character could also be maintained. That way if a character got tagged by another character one too many times it would go after the character, but if instead it was tagged by a character that it felt ambivalent toward it might instead go after another character that it was annoyed with.

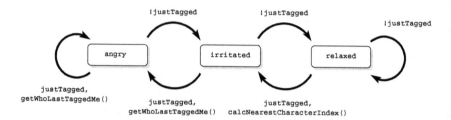

Figure 5.2. Simple FSM for the tag game.

If another character got tagged and instead of going after the near-est character it went for someone else, the spared character might reduce its anger toward that character. Or it might instead increase its feeling of friendliness toward that character and reciprocate the favor later on. Clearly the possibilities are endless.

From a game design perspective, mental state variables representing emotions usually have a pervasive influence on action selection. They are widely used in games to give an NPC moods, especially in games where you must look after the NPC's needs, for example, any game with some kind of virtual pet.

5.4.2   Finite-State Machines

A popular and convenient way to represent mental state variables is as Finite-State Machines (FSMs). Figure 5.2 shows a simple example FSM for the tag game. The nodes represent states and the arcs represent state-transitions. The event that triggers the transition is written on the arc, and following it is the output (if any) that occurs when the transition occurs. The start state is also an important part of the specification.

Just like decision trees, FSMs are intuitive and, with a suitable GUI, FSMs can be built and maintained by nonprogrammers. FSMs can easily be arranged in hierarchies in which each node can itself be a (hierarchical) FSM. FSMs can be augmented with timers to enable state transitions after a preprogrammed amount of time.

FSMs are also a convenient way to represent controllers that depend on any memory percept's value, not just mental state variables. For exam-ple, FSMs with states like "in attack mode" or "in following mode" are common. The states do not even have to be explicitly labeled as representing anything particular at all. FSMs are one of the most popular and well-documented techniques in game AI and this book's companion web site has links to some relevant articles (see also [HF03] and [Sam02]).

One of the key reasons FSMs are so useful is that an NPC can often be designed to have a single state variable whose value can be represented by the current node of the FSM. The inputs and outputs to the node then drive the character's behavior in that state. The downside of FSMs is that they can often get very complicated with a huge number of transitions and a proliferation of states.

5.4.3 Production Rules

Reactive production rules were introduced in Section 4.3 in the previous chapter. More generally, production rules are an important and convenient mechanism for creating general purpose controllers. In particular, they are well suited to implementing expert systems in which the game developer writes a Knowledge Base (KB) for how the character should behave. The KB can also be used to store, access, and manipulate a character's mental state using the convenient and powerful general purpose language of production rules.

When implementing production rule style systems using regular programming languages (like C/C++) *if*-statements, problems can arise when the number of rules becomes large. In particular, it can take a long time to test all the rules to see which ones fired. Therefore, special purpose production rule systems have been developed that use a fast algorithm (such as RETE) for matching the rules' firing conditions. They also have built-in support for conflict resolution when multiple rules match.

The first production rule system was called OPS5 and was invented in the early 1980s. Since then a number of other production rule systems have been created of varying degrees of sophistication [LNR87, SP96]. More recently, a language called RC++ was designed specifically for use in computer games. RC++ is a superset of C++ that adds the ability to specify production rules to control character behavior (or anything else for that matter). RC++ also provides a reactive subset for use with reactive controllers; more details and references can be found in [WM03].

5.4.4   Logical Inference

As a generalization of production rules, logical inference can obviously also be used to manage controller state. In particular, first-order logic can also be used to reason directly about the effects of actions, but the task is complicated by the fact that there is no inherent notion of change. One solution is to define a formal language within first-order logic called the *situation calculus* that includes a built-in notion of change. If you are interested in learning more about this approach see [Fun99, Rei01].

5.5   Communicating

Communicating between characters is useful and important for cooperating on tasks and formulating joint plans.[3] Communication also adds realism and highlights the AI by illustrating an NPC's internal mental state and thought processes.

In the simplest case, communication does not have to be verbal. For example, if a character is embarrassed, then the renderer can have access to this information so that its cheeks can be drawn in red. A player will see this and realize something about the NPC's internal state. Other NPCs should also be able to realize the NPC in question is embarrassed, but they cannot see and analyze the rendered image that the player sees. Therefore, the embarrassed NPC should directly broadcast how it is feeling to NPCs that are close enough and for whom it is otherwise reasonable, within the context of the game world, to expect them to know how the NPC is feeling.

Because of the current state of natural language processing, communicating from the player to the NPC is obviously hard. Typically the player communicates with NPCs through some simple (possibly voice-activated) menu system, or through button presses or gestures that have predefined meanings.

NPCs often communicate with players by using scripted dialog and cut scenes. A phrase of prescripted dialog can be treated as a speech action. Selecting which speech action to pick (if any) based on events in the game

---

[3]Although, unless NPCs have the ability and desire (i.e., they are on the team) to communicate, it is also unrealistic to assume that they would tell each other about their future plans.

world and an NPC's internal state can be performed using any of the techniques for building controllers described in this book. For example, in the tag game if an NPC starts being pursued it could say "Oh no, I'm being chased". If the NPC has a memory percept that records how many times it has been chased recently, the dialog could be more elaborate. For instance, if it has been chased a lot recently it could say something like "How come I'm the one who keeps getting chased?". While if it has not been chased much it could instead remark "Oh I thought you'd forgotten about me". More elaborate still is the case when an NPC has mental state variables like anger. An NPC can then utter phrases like "you're making me angry by keep chasing me", or "OK, that's it I'm going to get you back for this". Such comments can later make it clear to the player that the NPC they just tagged is not just chasing them by accident but is pursuing them to exact revenge. In contrast, without any dialog, all your hard AI programming work might go unnoticed and, more importantly, the player will not get the same immersive sense of the NPCs being alive.

From a game design perspective, care needs to be taken to avoid the dialog becoming boring or repetitive. This is often especially a problem when designing the controller for the NPC who plays the role of the commentator in a sports game. Typically, for any given situation, the commentator will randomly select one of several different appropriate pieces of dialog.

To generate more free-form dialog, you can use a text-to-speech engine, and the technology is getting to the point where it can be effective. In some games, the NPCs speak gibberish, but the tone is modulated according to how they are feeling.

For verbal communication between NPCs the ability to communicate does not have to be a literal one. It just means that it is plausible that they could communicate, for example, if they are nearby or if they are rendered to look like they are carrying some kind of communication device. For the sake of window dressing, you might like to have them appear to be speaking, but underneath the mechanism can be simpler. For example, NPCs can call the appropriate accessors on a controller class to return the value of various mental state variables. A more flexible approach is to use an explicit formal language. XML is a well-known example of a standard that is used to build formal language so that computers in the real world can communicate with each other in a flexible way.

In games, formal languages are also used for communicating among NPCs. To date, formal languages in games are often simpler than their XML-based real-world counterparts. The advantage of using even a simple formal language is that the game content does not have to be fixed in advance. Later on (even after the game ships), if new characters (or even inanimate objects) are added to the world they can communicate information about themselves to the existing NPCs. Provided the existing NPCs understand the same formal language they will know how to interact with the new object. The formal language can (as in [WW04]) even drive a text-to-speech engine to add the necessary window dressing to make it seem like they are talking.

5.6   Stochastic Controllers

As explained in Section 4.4.1 in the previous chapter, reactive stochastic controllers have no hysteresis and can result in NPCs who keep changing their minds. Adding state can therefore help enormously to make stochastic controllers more practical. In particular, if a controller is still in the middle of an action it can lower the probability that it will pick another action until it is finished. Once the action is finished it is free to pick randomly again. To avoid creating NPCs that are subject to rapid and violent mood swings the same idea can be used when selecting emotions. As a simple example, Listing 5.2 shows the calculation of an anger mental state variable such that there is an element of chance for whether the NPC gets angry when tagged, but once angry it stays angry until it tags someone else.

5.6.1   Hidden Markov Model

A Hidden Markov Model (HMM) is like an FSM with probabilities attached to the transition arcs and outputs. HMMs are so named because the states are hidden from the external observer and the transitions only depend on the current state (i.e., the Markov property). An HMM where the transitions depend on the state and the inputs is called an input-output HMM. If an arc corresponding to some input i leads from some state s to some new state s' and is labeled with probability p, then this means that

```
void tgControllerNPC::calcIsAngry()
{
    if (!perception->getAmITagged())
    { // If I'm not tagged then don't be angry
        isAngry = false;
        return;
    }

    // If I'm tagged and angry then stay angry
    if (isAngry) { return; }

    // If I'm tagged and not angry then there's a small chance I'll get angry
    tgReal probAngry = 0.1;

    // But if I just got tagged, then I get angry in proportion
    // to how often I've been tagged recently
    if (perception->getWasIJustTagged())
    {
        int const n = max(9, perception->getMyRecentTaggedCount());
        probAngry = tgReal(n)/10.0;
    }

    // Pick a random number uniformly between 0 and 1
    tgReal const r = tgMath::getRandom();
    if (r < probAngry) { isAngry = true; }
    else { isAngry = false; }
}
```

Listing 5.2. Stochastically calculate if NPC is angry.

the probability of making the transition given the input i is p:

$$P(s'|i, s) = p.$$

When the new state becomes s' there is also some probability q of outputting an action a:

$$P(a|s') = q.$$

Representing HMMs visually can be a bit confusing compared to a regular FSM because for each transition event there are multiple arcs (representing the different probabilities) going to multiple states. Writing a useful GUI is therefore more of a challenge, but see [aiS00] for an example of a tool for visualizing HMMs (and other graphical models).

An input-output HMM can be represented as a three-dimensional table, where the entry in table i, row j, column k corresponds to the probability of transitioning from state j to state k given the input i. If the HMM is in state j when an input i is received, then the k entries in table i, row j provide a probability distribution over possible next states. One of the methods in Appendix A is then used to pick the new state. To be complete, tables also need to be given for the probabilities of outputting actions in each state. As usual, one of the methods from Appendix A is used to pick an action from the probability distribution over actions associated with the new state.

HMMs are widely used as a representation in machine learning applications. Usually the structure of the HMM is given and the learning algorithm must determine the state-transition and action output probabilities that result in an output that matches the training examples. It is also possible to learn the structure of an HMM, but finding effective means for doing so is still an open research problem. To read more about HMMs, see [MS99].

Chapter 6

Searching

Despite their best efforts, controllers will sometimes pick actions that turn out to be a poor choice. Often it will only become apparent that an action was not the best choice after several more actions have been selected and executed. In such cases, it would be ideal if the game world could be set back to how it was before the (what turned out to be) undesirable action was selected. That way a different action could be picked and the whole process repeated until the best action choice was made. This chapter explains that, with certain caveats relating to speed, memory, and the extra knowledge a controller needs about the game world, it is possible for a controller to speculatively try out different action sequences until it finds a suitable one. In such cases, the controller is said to be searching for an action.

6.1 Discrete Tag Game

Section 2.1 in Chapter 2 introduced the tag game as a game that, from an AI perspective, was free of unimportant and distracting details. This chapter will (starting from Section 6.4) also use the tag game to explain how controllers can use search. But to explain the basic idea of search the tag game is too complicated to initially fulfill its pedagogical role. The problem is that search algorithms view change as a discrete phenomena so additional work is required to apply them to the continuous world of the tag game.

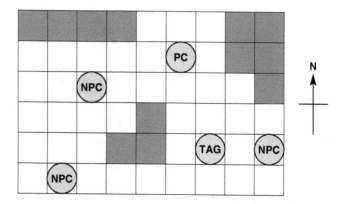

Figure 6.1. Scene from the discrete tag game.

The tag game can be turned into a simpler discrete version by assuming that all movement takes place on a discrete grid. The new game is referred to as the *discrete tag game* and Figure 6.1 shows a scene from the game. Assume each character can move up to one square at a time in any nondiagonal compass direction. Including staying still (denoted *U*), that gives five possible actions:

$$U : (0,0), N : (0,1), E : (1,0), S : (0,-1), W : (-1,0).$$

Adding the diagonals as directions to move or using a hexagonal is straightforward, and is left as an exercise to the reader. Removing the grid assumption is altogether more interesting and is covered later in Section 6.4. Note that there can be only one character in a cell at a time, and that a character is tagged if the tagged character is in a directly adjacent cell (i.e., diagonals do not count).

6.2 Controllers that Use Search

A controller that uses search to pick actions can simply try each possible action in turn and see which one turns out to be best. Figure 6.2 depicts the neighborhood around the tagged character in each of the five possible future game-states that arise from everyone else staying still while the tagged character is trying out each of its available actions. The assumption

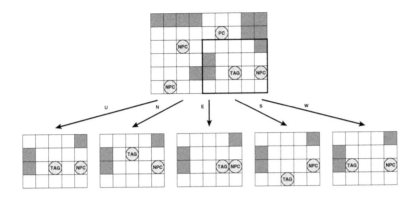

Figure 6.2. Five possible future game-states.

that everyone else stays still is a simplification that makes it easier to explain how search algorithms work. Later, in Section 6.6, the assumption is removed.

The maximum possible number of actions available to an NPC in any state is called the *branching factor*, so in the figure the branching facto is five.

The tagged character wants to end up in a cell next to an untagged character. Of the possible actions, the best one to pick is therefore E because, from the tagged character's point of view, it leads to a desirable outcome. A desirable game-state is referred to as a *goal* and is calculated by the percept calcIsGoal:

---

bool dtgPerception::calcIsGoal() **const**
{
    return 1 == getMyManhattanDistanceToNearestCharacter();
}

---

where the Manhattan distance d between two grid cells (p_x, p_y) and (q_x, q_y) is defined as

$$d = |p_x - q_x| + |p_y - q_y|.$$

The controller shown in Listing 6.1 searches for a goal one move ahead. To perform the search the controller needs access to the simulator, which is therefore passed in as a reference to itself when it calls the

```
void dtgControllerNPC::calcAction(int whoami, dtgSimulator& sim)
{
    perception->setMyIndex( whoami );
    // See Chapter 2 for a description of calcPossibleActions
    // Note: includes the null action (i.e., U in the text)
    sim.calcPossibleActions();
    vector<dtgAction> const& actions = sim.getPossibleActions();
    bool foundGoal = false;

    for (unsigned int i = 0; i < actions.size(); i++)
    {
        dtgSearchContext searchContext(&sim);
        searchContext.doAction(actions[i], whoami);
        if (perception->calcIsGoal())
        {
            foundGoal = true;
            action = actions[i];
            break;
        }
    }

    if (!foundGoal && !actions.empty())
    {
        action = actions[dtgMath::getRandomInt(actions.size())];
    }
}
```

Listing 6.1. Example of a simple one-step search.

controller's calcAction method. If the search fails, then the controller just picks an action randomly. A better alternative when a search fails is to use a heuristic to pick the "best" action; Section 6.4.1 describes the use of heuristics in more detail.

The dtgSearchContext object in Listing 6.1 is responsible for executing actions and then resetting the game-state back to how it was. Listing 6.2 shows the doAction method that records which actions are performed

---

```
void dtgSearchContext::doAction(dtgAction const& a, int const i)
{
    sim->doAction(a, i);
    actionList.push_back(a);
    identityList.push_back(i);
}

dtgSearchContext::~dtgSearchContext()
{
    while ( !actionList.empty() )
    {
        sim->undoAction(actionList.back(), identityList.back());
        actionList.pop_back();
        identityList.pop_back();
    }
}
```

Listing 6.2. Setting the game-state back to how it was.

and calls a corresponding method in the simulator. In particular, the simulator's doAction method provides a mechanism for performing speculative forward simulations outside the normal execution path. Executing an action with the doAction method alters the game-state, which can then be queried (through the perception object) to see if it is a goal.

The destructor of the dtgSearchContext class, also shown in Listing 6.2, is what resets the game-state back to how it was when the dtgSearch Context object was constructed. The simplest way for it to work is to make a copy of the game-state in its constructor and restore the copy in its destructor. An alternative solution, shown in the figure, requires no copying of the game-state object, uses no extra memory, and is therefore usually much faster. The idea is that the simulator has an undo method that gets called the required number of times in the dtgSearchContext's destructor. For the discretized tag game, writing an undo method is trivial, but for more complex games it can be time-consuming and error-prone. If you get it wrong, then a controller just thinking about what it wants to do can end up altering the actual state of the game world!

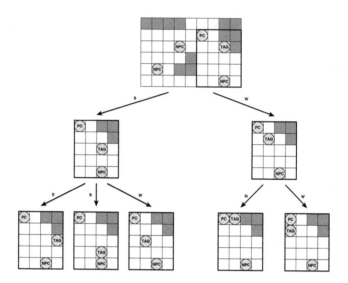

Figure 6.3. Doing and undoing actions.

Using the simulator to perform a search in the way just described is such a clever and powerful technique that it is important to appreciate its significance. In particular, the actual simulator for the game is being used as a proxy for the NPC's model of its world without affecting the real game-state.

If the perception object has internal state, then there also needs to be a mechanism to restore the original state after a search is finished. Otherwise a character thinking about what it wants to do can again lead to subtle AI bugs caused by the corruption of memory percepts.

6.3 Searching Further Ahead

The root of the tree in Figure 6.3 shows a different possible configuration of the discrete tag game in which no single action can result in a goal. The tagged character's controller therefore needs to search for a *sequence* of actions that lead to a goal. The search tree in the figure shows all future possible game-states that could arise from the tagged character moving two steps and (until Section 6.6) everyone else staying still. The search tree is a tool for thinking about search algorithms; practical algorithms do not explicitly build a search tree but simply explore it implicitly during their execution. There are some interesting points to observe about the search tree:

- only possible actions are shown. For example, in the initial configuration it is not possible to move N or E because there is an obstacle in the way; there are therefore no paths corresponding to moving N or E originating from the root node.

- no child nodes of a node x are shown if the child is the same node as x's parent. For example, the path S followed by N brings the tagged character back to where it just was. For the same reason no paths corresponding to the U action appear, since by staying still a character will, by definition, end up in the same grid cell. However, longer cycles are not removed, for example, the path W, S is shown even though it results in the same state as S, W on the other branch. At the possible cost of some extra memory required to remember some of the previously visited states, it is usually straightforward to detect and remove all repeated states.

- because repeated states are disallowed and the search space is finite, the search tree is finite. If repeated states are allowed, then the search tree would contain infinite branches such as $U, U, U, \ldots$ or $S, N, S, N, S, N, \ldots$. The search tree does nevertheless continue on much further than is shown in the figure.

- the search tree grows exponentially. Therefore, in the worst case, when there is no goal in the entire tree, a search can take an exponential amount of time because every single node has to be examined.

A sequence of actions that leads to a goal is called a *plan*. In the specific case where the goal is a location and a plan corresponds to a path to the goal, searching for a plan is called *path planning*. Since any game-state in which the tagged character is adjacent to any untagged character qualifies, there are many possible goals in Figure 6.3. For each goal, there are also many possible paths to reach it. For example, the path W, W leads to a goal and the path W, N leads to the same goal. There is only one plan

of length two that leads to the goal along the path *S, S*, but there are many
other longer plans that lead to the goal (not shown in the figure) such as
W, W, S, S, S, E.

6.3.1 Uninformed Search Algorithms

Uninformed search algorithms are simple search algorithms that, unlike
those described later in Section 6.4.1, do not use a heuristic to potentially
speed up the search. The algorithms can be used to search a tree like the
one in Figure 6.3 and are described in all introductory AI textbooks, in
many introductory computer science books, and on numerous web sites.
The section on search algorithms in [RN02] provides a particularly good
presentation.

The two basic uninformed search algorithms are breadth-first search
and depth-first search. Breadth-first search is guaranteed to find the shortest path to a goal but potentially uses an exponential (in the depth of the
tree) amount of memory to store instances of the game-state. Depth-first
search can be implemented using a simulator's undo mechanism to back-
track when it fails to find a goal and thus avoids storing (or copying) any
additional instances of the game-state. Even without an undo mechanism,
depth-first search can be implemented using only a linear (in the depth of
the tree) number of stored instances of the game-state. The downside of
depth-first search is that it is not guaranteed to find the shortest path. Moreover, on search trees that have infinite branches depth-first search can get
stuck in an infinite loop, but this can be remedied by placing an artificial
limit on the maximum depth of a search. Iterative deepening depth-first
search works by successively increasing the maximum search depth by
one each time until it finds a goal. For example, first it performs a depth-
first search on plans of length one, then (assuming it did not find a goal)
a depth-first search on plans of length two, then length three, and so on.
At the negligible cost, at least compared to the overall cost, of researching
the tree at previous depths, iterative deepening depth-first search is guaranteed to find an optimal plan and does not require an exponential amount
of memory.

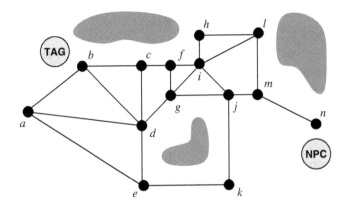

Figure 6.4. Waypoints for the original tag game.

6.4   Searching in Continuous Domains

Figure 6.4 shows a top-down view of a map from the original tag game (i.e., the one before the discrete version was introduced) overlaid with a collection of connected nodes, or a graph. The graph nodes are called *waypoints* and the lines indicate the ability of an NPC to move from one waypoint to another in a straight line without getting stuck on any obstacles. The waypoint graph provides a discrete representation, of the underlying continuous map,[1] which is suitable to apply search algorithms to. Of course, the absence of a connection between two nodes does not necessarily imply that an NPC cannot travel between them. If an NPC has another controller that does not employ path planning it can use that and completely ignore the waypoints. The waypoints simply represent the option to use path planning in a continuous domain, for example, to plan a path to a faraway goal that is hidden from view.

Figure 6.4 also shows the tagged character and an NPC. If the tagged character wants to move toward the current NPC's position, it first needs to compute the closest waypoint to its current position (i.e., node b) and the closest waypoint to its goal position (i.e., node n). It can then use any search algorithm it pleases to search the graph to find a path from b to

---

[1]The map is continuous in the sense that it is meant to represent a continuous domain. Obviously it is still ultimately implemented on a digital computer using floating-point numbers.

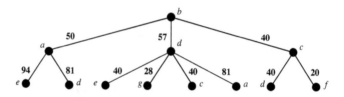

Figure 6.5. Searching the waypoint graph.

n. For example, it might find the path *b*, *c*, *f*, *i*, *j*, *m*, *n*. Once it has computed a path, the tagged character can use a path-following subcontroller
to smoothly reach its destination. Path following is another example of a
simple steering behavior like those described in Section 4.2 in Chapter 4,
and can be implemented easily using the pursue/seek controller.

The two separate levels of, first, path planing using the discrete waypoint representation, and second, path following using the underlying continuous representation, can be implemented in a variety of ways. For example, looking back at Figure 2.2 in Chapter 2 there are possibly multiple
levels of simulators and controllers. For path planning in the tag game the
simulator mentioned in the figure is obviously the regular tag game simulator, and the approximate simulator is for the waypoint grid. For example,
if the search is currently considering node *a*, then the approximate simulator is responsible for generating the possible successor nodes *b*, *d*, and
e. The approximate simulator is so simple that it might be overkill to refer
to it as a simulator at all. It certainly need not be implemented with the
formality of defining an approximate simulator class, approximate game-
state, etc. In particular, the approximate simulator can just be represented
as the method in the search algorithm that is responsible for generating,
from a given waypoint node, successor nodes to search.

6.4.1 Informed Search

In the discrete tag game each grid cell can be thought of as a waypoint,
where each waypoint is connected to its four neighbors and itself. Therefore, searching the waypoint graph is similar to searching in the discrete
tag game, and Figure 6.5 shows the first two steps in the corresponding
search tree. The numbers on the arcs correspond to the distances (rounded
to the nearest integer) between nodes and in general are referred to as *costs*.

The total cost of a path to the current node x is denoted $g(x)$; for example, the cost to get to node e along the path b, d, e is

$$g(e) = 57 + 40 = 97.$$

Note that, because the NPC is no longer searching on a regular grid, the optimal path to the goal is not necessarily coincident with the path with the shortest number of steps. For example, the path b, c, f, i, j, m, n is clearly shorter than the path b, d, e, k, m, n even though it contains more steps. This means that breadth-first search is no longer guaranteed to find the optimal path, but a simple generalization called uniform cost search will.

Informed search methods are characterized by the use of a heuristic function h that attempts to estimate the cost of the cheapest path to the goal from any given node x. Combined with the known cost to reach the current node x, this gives an estimate for the cheapest cost to reach the goal through the node x as

$$f(x) = g(x) + h(x). \tag{6.1}$$

If the heuristic function makes a reasonable guess at the true remaining cost to the goal it is useful during the search because the most promising paths can be explored first. As a special case, if the heuristic function was always exactly right (i.e., it was an oracle), then following it would result in taking the optimal path to the goal without any need to search alternatives paths.

The most well-known and widely used informed search algorithm is called A⋆. If the heuristic function used with A⋆ is always optimistic about the expected cost to the goal, then A⋆ is guaranteed to find the optimal path. An optimistic heuristic function is said to be admissible, and the Euclidean distance between two nodes qualifies as an admissible heuristic in the tag game.

For any given admissible heuristic, no other algorithm will explore less of the search tree than A⋆ and still be guaranteed to find the optimal path. A⋆ is thus as good an optimal search algorithm as there is, which explains why it is so popular. You can read more about the theoretical properties of A⋆ in [Pea84, RN02]; there are also a great many articles about how to implement A⋆ to be found in the game AI literature. One interesting article

[Rab00] examines the practical consequences of relaxing the requirement that the heuristic function be admissible. There are many online resources, including source code, devoted to search algorithms in general, and A⋆ in particular. This book's companion web site has pointers to such resources.

A problem with using the standard A⋆ algorithm for games is that in the worst case it requires an exponential amount of memory. A simple modification called iterative-deepening A⋆ reduces the memory requirements at the cost of potentially reexploring parts of the search tree. Other more recent and complicated algorithms like memory-bounded A⋆ and simplified memory-bounded A⋆ are described in [RN02]. See [AL98] for an article about using A⋆ with partially ordered "soft" constraints.

6.4.2 Replanning

When an NPC starts following a path that was computed by applying a search algorithm to the waypoint graph, unexpected events will inevitably occur. That is because the waypoint graph is just a discrete approximation to the real underlying continuous game world. The game world could have all sorts of complicated physics that are not captured in the waypoint graph. For example, an object not even represented in the waypoint graph could fall over or explode and debris could block the preplanned path. The preplanned path also does not take into consideration low-level behaviors, like collision avoidance routines, that can override other behaviors and could easily become activated to cause the path to deviate from the anticipated one.

The consequence of all this uncertainty is that a plan cannot be followed blindly. Lower-level controllers, like collision avoidance behaviors, constantly need to be active. The world can diverge so quickly from how it was when a plan was computed that in practice a plan is almost never executed to completion. Instead, it is periodically discarded and a new plan that takes into account the updated state of the game world is computed. This is called replanning and how often it needs to be done depends on how accurate an approximation the waypoint graph is to the real underlying game world. Although replanning has to be done regularly it does not usually have to be done so regularly that the search calculation cannot be spread across several frames.

Later, in Section 6.6.1, replanning is explored in more detail in the context of the additional uncertainty that arises from taking into account the possible future actions of other characters.

6.5 Waypoints

Waypoints are usually added to a map by a level designer. There are also automatic procedures to generate waypoints, for example, the Area Awareness System (AAS) described in [vW01].[2] The AAS also supports fast computation of the nearest waypoint to a given position, which can otherwise be a significant time cost. One of the disadvantages of automatic waypoint placement is that waypoints do not always end up in the ideal location. That is, waypoint placement is something of an art and a good level designer will take care to place waypoints near interesting features in the game world that an automatic system might not be able to recognize as important.

Waypoints can also be annotated with additional information like the affordances described in Section 3.3.3 in Chapter 3. For example, a waypoint can be annotated with whether it is a good sniping location, so that an NPC that wants to do some sniping can then calculate the nearest suitable waypoint and plan a path to get there. In the tag game, waypoints could be annotated to state if they make a good hiding position. Hiding information depends on the current location of the tagged character, so a waypoint would have to be annotated with a list of waypoints from which it is hidden. To determine a hiding spot an NPC could then pick the nearest waypoint that is hidden from the nearest waypoint to the tagged character. For example, in Figure 6.4, node b is the nearest node to the tagged character and node k is the closest to the NPC that is hidden from b.

Using annotations to place knowledge in the environment at design time, versus having NPCs figure it out at runtime, represents a trade-off between flexibility and speed [Doy02]. In particular, with a lot of knowledge embedded in the environment, NPCs themselves do not need the flexibility afforded to them by sophisticated AI algorithms. At runtime they can thus make decisions much faster. With AI routines usually given no more than

---

[2]See [KL00] for a different approach to the path planning problem, from robotics research, that skips the need for waypoints.

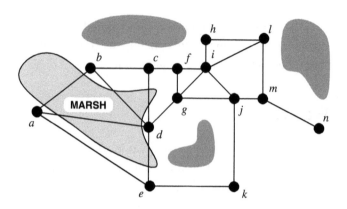

Figure 6.6. Marsh land is expensive to cross.

10% of the CPU per cycle (and often less), game designers therefore usually spend a lot of time and effort on annotating the game world. But, as computers get faster, more of the work can reasonably be done at runtime by the AI algorithms.

Some information that a game can use to annotate waypoints is only available at runtime. For example, if there was enough time and memory, a memory percept could record for each waypoint a list of characters that had been within visual range of the waypoint. That way an NPC would only be permitted to use the portion of the waypoint network consistent with its past experiences.

6.5.1 Tactical Path Planning

Not only can waypoints themselves be annotated, but so can the arcs between them. For example, in Figure 6.6 some marshland has been added to the tag game world. Unlike an obstacle, marsh land is traversable but suppose it multiplies the usual time cost due to distance ten-fold. The result is that if an NPC wanted to go from node a to node d it would be cheaper to take the path a, e, k, j, g, d rather than go directly and have to venture through the marsh.

In general, annotations on waypoint arcs can be computed automatically provided a rule is given for how terrain and nearby objects affect the cost. Common causes of increased cost are nearby guard towers or regions vulnerable to snipers. Arc costs can also be computed dynamically in real-time depending on the location of enemies and allies. In [RG03] arc costs are increased along paths with fallen comrades since they clearly represent undesirable routes. If the arc costs do vary significantly it will obviously invalidate any plan computed with the old costs and a replanning step will be necessary. The arc costs can also vary according to character type. For example, some characters might travel through water more easily than across dry land and so should associate different costs with submerged arcs to characters that do not like to get their feet wet. You can read more about tactical path planning in [vdS02].

Increasing arc costs to influence behavior must be done with care because in practice the efficient operation of A⋆ depends on the heuristic function not being too optimistic. For example, if the heuristic function is always zero (maximally optimistic), then A⋆ reduces to uniform cost search, which is slow and uses a lot of memory. So the higher the arc costs, the more relatively optimistic the heuristic becomes and the longer the search algorithm takes. Of course, a controller can also modify the heuristic to reduce its optimism but if it goes too far, so that it becomes pessimistic, you can end up with stupid NPCs that take noticeably suboptimal paths.

6.6 Adversarial Search

The examples used up until now in this chapter, of the tagged character using search to plan a path to the nearest untagged character, have a serious flaw: they all assume that the other characters being chased stay still! Clearly, if a character saw the tagged character heading toward it, it would run away. If the tagged character blindly followed the path it had planned based on the original position, by the time it reached its destination the untagged character would be long gone.

However, if the tagged character does not wait until it has finished executing its plan, but replans part way through, the situation is slightly improved. Now, provided replanning is frequent enough, the tagged character will always (more or less) be heading toward the untagged character. If the tagged character is a lot faster it should eventually catch the untagged character, but if they are about the same speed, then it will just chase the untagged character around and not necessarily get any closer. A better solution would be if the tagged character could anticipate the untagged character's future position and plan a path to arrive at where it thinks it will be instead of where it is right now. That way it could plan to cut the untagged character off, as shown later in Figure 6.8.

One way to anticipate the untagged character's future behavior is to use adversarial search techniques that come from the academic field of game theory [Osb03, RN02]. The idea is that there is some notion of a score that one character is trying to maximize and the other character is trying to minimize. In the tag game example, the distance between the tagged character and a given character can be used as the "score", in which case, the tagged character is trying to minimize the score and the untagged character to maximize it.

When the tagged character is deciding where to move it assumes the untagged character is rational (see Section 6.6.1 for some other possibilities) and will always pick its move to maximize the score (i.e., the separation distance). Given the move that represents the untagged character's rational choice, the tagged character then picks a move to minimize the score. Figure 6.7 shows the first layer (or ply) in the adversarial search tree that corresponds to the discrete tagged game shown in Figure 6.1. In the figure only one other character's moves are shown, but in general it should include all the possible moves of all the other characters. Clearly, with all the additional possibilities provided by the other player's moves, the adversarial search tree expands faster than that in Figure 6.2.

In Figure 6.1, the NPC shown cannot move E because it is already at the Eastern edge of the grid. The reason it cannot also move W after the tagged character has moved E is due to the assumption of only one character per grid cell. Since characters move simultaneously the choice to let the tagged character occupy the disputed cell is arbitrary and up to the simulator to decide. Notice the U move, to move nowhere, is important in an adversarial search because if the tagged character decides an untagged character's best move is to move next to it, then it obviously wants to stay where it is.

Ideally the adversarial search tree would be expanded out until all the leaves have been resolved and one or another character has won. In the tag game the tagged character wins if it catches the untagged character. The cases when the untagged character has not been caught could potentially go on forever, but there may be cycles that it can stick to without ever being caught. Or the game could dictate that the tagged character loses if

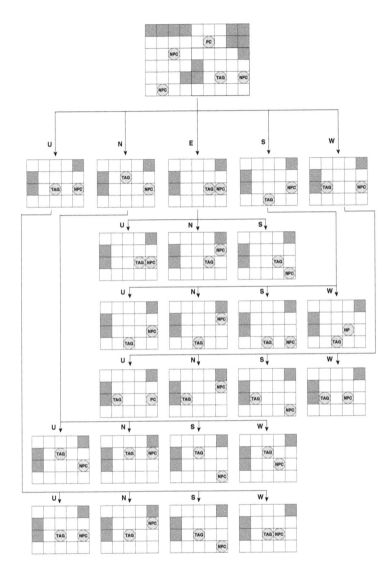

Figure 6.7. Adversarial search tree.

it has not caught a character in a certain number of moves. Regardless, it is usually infeasible to search all the way to resolution for all but the simplest games. In particular, the adversarial search tree is usually so large that an NPC must artificially restrict the number of ply it can look ahead. The value of the leaves of the tree can then be evaluated based on the score at that point.[3]

Once the score at the leaves has been determined the values are backed up using the min-max algorithm. The min-max algorithm assumes that one player (in this case the tagged character) picks the move that minimizes the score and the other (the untagged character) picks to maximize the score. More details about the algorithm, and alpha-beta pruning that can speed it up, can be found in [Osb03, RN02].

Adversarial search works well for board games, but there are a number of factors that limit its usefulness more generally in computer games:

- if the tagged character and the untagged character are both NPCs there does not have to be any guesswork about what each one will do; they can simply ask each other. This does, however, raise a new set of issues addressed in Section 6.6.1.

- if one of the characters is the player character, assuming it will play rationally can make NPCs over-cautious. That is, by always planning for the worst case scenario an NPC can make for a very boring opponent.

- for the discrete tag game the adversarial search is reasonable. But as pointed out in Section 6.4.2 the waypoint grid is just a rough approximation to the game world in the regular tag game. Therefore, after a couple of plays, an adversarial search's view of the game world is likely to have diverged so far from what would really happen that it is unlikely to be useful. Unfortunately, this is a difficult problem because if there is no way to search very deeply the technique is probably not reliable in the first place.

6.6.1 Treating Adversaries as Part of the Environment

An alternative to adversarial search is to treat other characters as part of the environment. This means that when searching forward an adversary's

---

[3]Some games do not have a score until the end when someone wins or loses. But it is usually straightforward to invent a heuristic that measures how well each player is doing that can act as the "score" before the game is finished.

action choices are determined by some other mechanism. For example, a controller could be used as a predictor percept to predict an action.

Section 3.5 in Chapter 3 already explained why it is sometimes not possible, or desirable, to use an NPC's actual controller as a predictor percept for how it will behave in future. But in light of Section 6.4.2, the point about the use of an approximate simulator should be clearer. In particular, if the adversarial search is using an approximate simulator, then an adversary's actual controller cannot be used directly because it is only compatible with the real game simulator. However, if the adversary has a high-level controller that can interact with the approximate simulator, then that could be used instead. But the results will not be completely reliable because it is still only the approximate simulator that is being used.

A more sophisticated alternative (also alluded to in Section 3.5) is to simulate forward the whole game loop, i.e., pick a high-level discrete action, translate the high-level action down to appropriate game actions, and execute the game actions up to the point where the adversary's action choice is required. At that point the adversary's real controller is used to provide a prediction about which action it will pick that is (subject to the influence of the player character) guaranteed to be correct. To find the best action choice, the process can be repeated for all the high-level actions the controller is considering. The process can also obviously be applied repeatedly to search further into the future. Of course, if the adversary is also using a similar search as part of its decision-making process, then care must be taken to avoid getting stuck in an infinite loop.

By using a suitable controller as a stand-in for the player, the player character can also be treated as part of the environment during a search. Creating a controller that is accurate enough to be a useful stand-in can require online learning (see Section 7.2 in the next chapter), but an existing NPC's controller might suffice.

Before proceeding with an example, it is important to fully appreciate that treating an adversary as part of the environment means the search only considers one possible action that an adversary might choose. In contrast, an adversarial search explicitly considers all the adversaries' possible actions. Note that, even if a predictor percept is written to return a probability distribution over possible actions as an answer to which action a character will pick, this still qualifies as treating the character as part of the environment. That is because in the adversarial search nothing is assumed about which action the character will pick, indeed it is part of the min-max algorithm's job to figure it out. But if the probabilities are supplied, then the information is already fixed and there is nothing for the adversarial search to calculate.[4] In fact, the case where a single action is chosen as a character's future action is just a special case in which all the probability is assigned to one action.

In [Fun99] there is an example of using search (limited to looking only six moves ahead), in which the adversaries are treated as part of the environment, to implement herding behavior. The example can easily be recast in the context of the tag game as the problem of getting the tagged character to herd the untagged characters into some corner of the game world. Presumably this would be a good tactic for increasing the odds of tagging someone.

Figure 6.8 illustrates how intermittent replanning, with the goal of getting more untagged characters heading in the desired direction (in this case the upper left corner), leads to herding behavior. In particular, the desired effect of the tagged character getting in and around the untagged characters to frighten them in the right direction emerges automatically. The tagged character uses a simple model of how the untagged characters will move to anticipate their future positions. In particular, it knows the untagged characters are afraid of it and will run in the opposite direction if it gets too close. It does not model their collision avoidance behavior and thus an unanticipated near-collision between the two untagged characters results in what actually happens when the plan is executed diverging from what the tagged character planned.

6.7 Rendering a Search

Search is being presented as a tool that can be used by a controller to pick actions. In this context, the only visible part of the search is the end re-

---

[4]In games that include an element of chance the min-max algorithm can be modified to use expected score. But this is still not the same as supplying a probability distribution for the character's action choices. The difference is that the probability used to calculate the expected score is the probability of different outcomes due to uncertain game world physics and not uncertainty about which action the character will choose. Once the expected score of each move has been calculated the rational character modeled in the adversarial search will, with absolute certainty, pick the move with the best expected outcome.

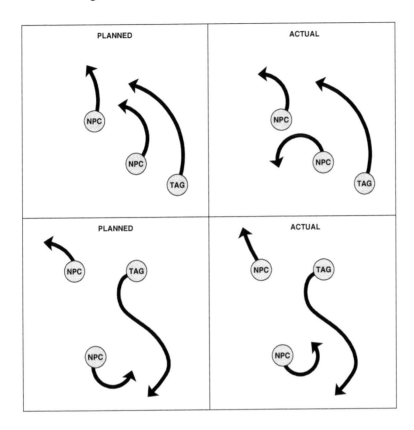

Figure 6.8. Herding using replanning.

sult: the action that the character decides to perform. The search process itself takes place inside the character's head and an external observer has no way to tell that search is being to used to pick actions or not. Of course, if the search takes a long time, then there may be a visible pause while the character thinks about what to do. If a character takes a particularly long time to search, an animation of it scratching its head might be appropriate.[5] While this might hint at the internal mechanism being used by the controller, the search itself is still hidden.

There are, however, occasions when the search process itself is rendered. This can be because the game designer wants to explicitly dramatize an NPC trying to figure something out, or simply as the by-product

---

[5] As pointed out earlier, the search cost can usually be spread across several frames.

of the player character trying to solve a problem. For example, consider a character stuck in a maze and trying to get out. The character could be the player character (in which case the human is directing the search) or an NPC. By rendering the game-state as the character tries different paths through the maze, an animation of the search process is created. The case when the search is not rendered is analogous to a character having a map of the maze. The map is searched in advance to find a way out, and only then does the character start to move. The resulting animation would (assuming the map was accurate) be of the character simply walking out of the maze without making any mistakes or detours.

When a search is rendered, undoing actions (when they do not lead to goals) means performing in-game actions that get the world back to how it was. For example, if a character in a maze finds a dead end, then it has to walk back to some previous point in the search. Note that, the game-state may represent quantities like time and fatigue, in which case, the game-state can only be put back to approximately how it was because time will have passed and the character will be more tired.

As explained in Section 6.2, when a search is not rendered, if an action sequence turns out to be no good, then, instead of undoing it with more in-game actions, the current game-state is either reversed with a special undo action or discarded and a saved one restored. For a rendered search, NPCs cannot revert to a previous game-state if the player has already seen or felt the consequences of subsequent actions. At least, it would make for a frustrating (although perhaps fairer) game-play experience if the world kept popping back to how it was for the convenience of an NPC.

For human players there are less restrictions on resetting the game-state. Human players can usually save games in some kind of permanent storage, which leads to a crude, but widely used, form of search in which the player can revert to a save point whenever something disastrous happens. Upon resuming the game the player will choose some alternative course of action that hopefully has more desirable consequences. Many games automatically save at key points; there are also often restrictions placed on the number and location of save points. Although it is interesting to imagine if it were otherwise, usually games do not model the frustration NPCs might feel about having the world reset whenever the player character is doing badly. On the contrary, NPCs are invariably kept blissfully ignorant that the world has been reset at all.

6.8 General Goal Action Planning

This chapter has emphasized path planning as an application of search. This is because path planning is widely used in games, and simple extensions like tactical path planning can yield a wide variety of impressive behaviors. Because it is clear which actions and percepts are relevant, path planning problems are relatively simple.

In the real world, there are much more complex planning problems where the relevant actions and percepts are not at all obvious. For example, even something seemingly simple like trying to catch a bus involves figuring out the solution to many subproblems at many different levels of abstraction. There can also be trade-offs that need to be resolved between multiple competing goals, such as the goal to eat versus the goal to catch the bus.

To describe planning problems, languages such as the Planning Domain Definition Language (PDDL), have been invented. They help the problem to be carefully specified, heuristics to be automatically generated, and the problem to be automatically broken down into subtasks and (hopefully) solved.

In computer games there are also complex planning problems that are often presented in the form of puzzles for the player to figure out. For example, a common scenario in a game is a locked door. The player might be expected to infer (using commonsense knowledge about locks and keys) that they need to find a key. They then formulate a high-level plan to go and find the key, come back, and open the door. Each of the steps in the plan is a planning problem in and of itself. Finding the key involves formulating a plan to search some portion of the game world. Subtactical path planning problems like walking across a room unnoticed, say, and staying close to cover might present themselves. Once the key is found a plan to get back to the locked door is needed.

Although computer games contain complex planning problems it is often the player's job to figure them out. NPCs usually only need to solve simpler path planning problems that might arise during the execution of the player's high-level plan. Even if the player needs some help, it is easier to simply give them prescribed hints, which is possible because the game designer who thought up the puzzle in the first place also thought of how it would be solved.

In the tag game the problem of deciding which waypoint is the goal is a high-level control problem. But it does not really require planning, instead controllers like the ones described in Section 5.4 in the previous chapter would be appropriate. For example, if the tagged character is angry with a particular character, then its goal should be the waypoint closest to that character. Or better still, the goal should be to head toward the waypoint that it believes will end up being the closest to the object of its anger a couple of moves in the future. If the tagged character is not angry, then its goal is the waypoint that gets it closest to any untagged character. Selecting goals for the untagged characters is equally as straightforward. There simply needs to be a controller to decide whether to run away, or whether to hide.

If the tag game was extended so that, for example, characters could move obstacles around to build and dismantle barricades of different shapes and forms, then it could be made equivalent to the classic blocks world planning domain. The addition of weapons that require ammunition can result in planning problems that are analogous to the problem (mentioned earlier) of finding a key for a lock. If there are a lot of objects that require various resources to make them work, and getting those resources entails finding resources for other objects, then it might be reasonable to consider using a planner. But if there are only a few resource-driven objects, it is better to just write simple *if-then* rules such as "if the gun is empty, then look for ammunition". The NPC then blindly follows the rules without any understanding of what it is trying to achieve. But the resulting behavior obviously looks no different than the case where a sophisticated planner figured out from first principles that in order to kill its enemy it needed a loaded gun.

There is a lot of interesting literature on planning, for example, the work done on real-time planning for NASA's Deep Space One mission [MNPW98]. There is also some exciting work that has been done using stochastic search to quickly (on average) solve complex planning problems [KS96, KS03]. Once again, see [RN02] for a thorough overview of the subject.

Chapter 7

Learning

Machine learning promises to play a prominent role in helping game AI scale up to more complex game worlds. But to date machine learning has only been used sporadically in computer games, so this chapter is therefore more speculative than the others. It is also more technically challenging, but by the end you should at least have gained some important intuitions. As usual, plenty of references are provided to help you follow up on any topics of interest.

There are a lot of potential applications of machine learning to games, but in any industry there is a natural resistance to using new technology, so this chapter takes a conservative approach. In particular, the emphasis is on machine learning techniques that do not necessarily have a major impact on game design, and that a game developer can easily experiment with by themselves. As such, this chapter only skims the surface of what is possible, but will hopefully whet your appetitive for this exciting and important subject.

7.1 Simulated Learning

Although machine learning has not been used widely in games, there are numerous games in which characters appear to learn. The effect is typically achieved by having a character slowly reveal information that they already possessed when the game shipped. The order, or nature, of the information revealed sometimes depends on interaction with the player. A related trick is to impair a character in some way (as is done with different difficulty settings) and have the character slowly improve over time by reducing the level of impairment.

Players also often associate stateful controllers that simply remember past information with learning. For example, an NPC in a game might ask a player her name. When the NPC later refers to the player by name you might say the NPC has "learned" her name.

None of these simulated learning techniques would qualify as machine learning in the academic sense, but they are simple and can be surprisingly effective from the player's point of view. Before embarking on applying machine learning to your game it is therefore important to consider whether simulated learning could be used instead. The main reason why "real" learning might be required is if it would produce a better quality solution than hand coding, or if a character has to learn something at runtime from a source of information (such as the person who bought the game) that is unavailable at development time.

7.2   Definitions

The controllers that have been described in earlier chapters are all intended to be defined by the game developer according to some internal notion of how they think an NPC should behave. In contrast, learning a controller requires a developer to be much more explicit about how an NPC should behave. This usually involves giving the NPC examples of how to behave, or giving it rewards when it does the right thing. Giving an NPC examples of how to behave is called *supervised learning*, while providing rewards is referred to as *unsupervised learning*. Unsupervised learning is so named because an NPC must largely figure out for itself how to behave in order to receive the rewards.

Another important distinction is whether the learning takes place *online* or *offline*.[1] Online learning takes place in real-time while the game is being played, while offline learning takes place as a batch processing step that occurs when the game is not being played.

---

[1]In the context of machine learning, the terms "online" and "offline" should not be confused with their more conventional meanings in terms of networks. The two uses of the words are unrelated; online and offline learning can take place regardless of whether the player is online (in the network sense) or not.

A common misconception about machine learning is that most of the effort goes into the machine learning algorithms. Although the algorithms are obviously important, the real effort usually goes into crafting the percepts that act as the data for the machine learning algorithm. Unfortunately, getting the percepts right is a difficult subject to write about. The problem is that each learning problem usually requires its own unique set of percepts. There are, however, some common patterns and it turns out that many of these have already been covered in Chapter 3 and Chapter 5. That is, the percepts that would be useful for you to write a controller are often the same ones that would be useful to a machine learning algorithm. For example, your controller code will usually be a lot simpler if you use percepts that calculate relative coordinates instead of global coordinates. Similarly, for a machine learning algorithm, the learning problem will usually be a lot simpler (i.e., you will need less data) if it has access to relative coordinates. Think of the machine learning algorithm as trying to write the controller code instead of you. If you imagine you would have to write an extremely complicated controller to figure out the correct action, given the available percepts, then chances are the learning algorithm will fail dismally. Any percept you define to make the problem simpler is therefore a good thing. There are many good books about machine learning; for example, see [Mit97, DHS00, HTF01, RN02]. For a less technical introduction, see [WF99]. There are also a number of articles that have specifically addressed learning in games and game-like worlds, for example see [BDI+02, Ale02, Man03, DEdGD04].

7.2.1 Offline Unsupervised Learning

From a technical perspective, the attractive property of online learning is that the player can be involved in the process, which can lead to some exciting AI effects. But because the learning directly impacts the player's experience of the game the decision to use online learning has ramifications for game design. Shipping a game that includes online learning also requires confidence that the algorithms are robust enough to provide a quality experience no matter what (within reason) a player does. Finally, the learning has to be shoehorned into the often tight CPU and memory budgets available for the game AI. Online learning is therefore a challenging way to introduce learning into games, requiring many advanced tricks from machine learning that are still proprietary and beyond the scope of an introductory book like this one.

That leaves offline learning. The advantage of offline learning is that it can be applied before the game ships and so fits in with a game's standard quality assurance process. If the learned controllers are not good enough they can be relearned, or if necessary dropped entirely and (at the expense of all the wasted effort on learning) replaced by hand-coded ones. The CPU and memory constraints are also more lax as all the hard work is done before the game ships. The downside of offline learning is that there is no way for a player to necessarily be able to tell whether a controller for an NPC was learned or written by hand. The NPCs the player encounters in the game have no ability to learn, it is just that learning was possibly used to create their controllers. The learning is simply being used as a means to an end, as an alternative method for creating controllers.

Offline learning's apparent major benefit is therefore that it can act as a labor-saving device for developers. Instead of needing to hand-craft a controller for an NPC, the NPC can learn how to behave on its own. In reality, the process is far from as magical as it sounds and involves hours of hard work to get the learning to produce an acceptable controller. It is probably better to think of offline learning as a tool for mass producing (at least in the long term) higher quality AI that can better interact with more complex game worlds. When learning works correctly, the jump in quality can be by orders of magnitude. The reason is that, by automating the process of producing controllers, the scale of problems that can be tackled, the generality, and the robustness all improve. In that sense it is similar to other forms of automation. The first time an automated assembly plant for making cars (or anything else) was created it probably took more time and effort than it would have to simply make the object by hand. The benefits come much later when the manufacturing process has been refined. Once machine learning techniques become established in the games industry, the quality and range of AI in games should see a similar transformation. In all likelihood, machine learning will come to dominate game AI in much the same way as it has come to dominate academic AI.

Having established offline learning as worthy of further interest, the question remains about whether to use supervised learning or unsupervised learning. Aside from the technical differences, the biggest practical impediment to using supervised learning in game development is that it requires a data set to learn from. Where will this data set come from? Academic researchers stumble across the same problem when developing new machine learning algorithms. They have therefore set up a machine learning repository [BM98] that includes a number of data sets that can be used for comparing and evaluating algorithms. But there is no such repository of data sets for your game, so you would have to create one! That can be a tremendous amount of work, especially if you are inexperienced at doing it. You have to decide what data to collect, who is going to generate it, how much data you need, how to store it, how to clean it up, and much much more. In addition, every time the game's physics changes (which it is likely to do all the time during production) you might have to regenerate all the data. To have even a chance success, a supervised learning project would therefore probably require coordination between the whole development team.

In contrast, unsupervised learning only requires access to standard computing resources and the programming resources of an individual or small team. When the game physics changes, a controller might still need to be relearned but, if everything is set up right, it should be just a matter of rerunning the learning.

There are also some strong precedents for the successful application of unsupervised offline learning to games, one of the most well-known of which is in traditional board games where the TD-Gammon program used a version of *reinforcement learning* to learn to play backgammon [Tes95]. The program learned to play at the level of the world's best human experts simply by playing millions of games against itself. Previous attempts to hand-code solutions had failed to produce anything more than programs that were mediocre players. Reinforcement learning has also been successfully used in video games like Ratbag games' "Dirt Track Racing". Reinforcement learning is therefore the focus of this chapter.

7.3 Rewards

In what follows, a controller that can learn is referred to as a *learner*. Once a learner has finished learning it reverts to a being regular controller. A learner may also be referred to as a controller when (often as part of the learning algorithm) it is being used in its role as a controller. The difference between a learner and a controller is that a learner can modify the function it computes between percepts and actions. In order to modify the function so that the learner improves it needs some kind of feedback on how it is doing. There also has to be some initial unlearned controller to bootstrap the process; for example, the random controller introduced in Section 4.1.1 in Chapter 4 could be used.

In the previous chapter on searching, goals and costs can be thought of as providing a type of feedback. Cost is negative feedback and reaching a goal is positive feedback. In this chapter, rewards are introduced as a unifying concept that is used to provide explicit feedback to a controller. Negative rewards correspond to punishment and positive rewards to encouragement. Rewards can come from a variety of sources, such as the game itself, or from another player. Like goals, rewards are implemented as percepts. For example, in the tag game, a positive reward would be granted to the tagged character upon tagging another character. At every step when the tagged character fails to tag another character it would receive no reward, or possibly even a negative reward.

Since the reward percept is defined by the game developer it provides a lot of control, albeit somewhat indirect, over the NPC's personality. That is, the conditions of the reward are like high-level goals or the "ends". The reinforcement learning algorithm must then work out the best "means" to receive the rewards. For example, to make an NPC that likes to get revenge, the associated learner could receive an extra reward for tagging a character with whom the NPC is angry. However, depending on the relative weighting assigned to different rewards and punishments, this scheme could backfire. For example, an NPC might learn to deliberately make itself angry by letting itself be tagged repeatedly by the same character just so it can get angry, and receive the extra reward from tagging it back. It might even chase the tagged character around trying to get itself tagged! Since the learning algorithm has no way to know the underlying intent behind the reward function, it will simply try to exploit the environment in any way it can to receive the reward.

Clearly coming up with a reward that yields the desired behavior can require some ingenuity. For example, researchers have struggled for a long time with how to use rewards and learning to automatically generate realistic-looking motion. Initial attempts rewarded the distance traveled in a fixed time period which led to some realistic motions and a lot of comical-looking ones. Modifying the reward function to include terms for smoothness and symmetry helped tilt the scales more toward aesthetically pleasing motion. But it was only recently, in [LCR03], that the insightful discovery was made that rewarding motion that is resilient to noisy sensors is one of the most effective strategies.

If tweaking the reward to get the desired behavior starts to become a painstaking and frustrating experience it is worth questioning whether the behavior you want is so specific that it might be easier to hand-code it.

7.3.1 Utility

Whenever an NPC has to make a decision, there are a number of possible actions it can take, some of which may result in positive rewards and some in negative rewards. What makes the problem of choosing actions interesting is that some of the actions that result in an immediate negative reward may ultimately lead to a large positive reward. The task of the NPC is to learn which actions are most likely to lead to large rewards in the long run. This is somewhat similar to the case of searching, where the action that takes an NPC closer to its goal (in terms of Euclidean distance) may ultimately lead to a dead end. That is, the optimal path may sometimes momentarily appear to lead away from the goal.

The idea of long-term reward is captured in the notion of utility. Utility is defined as the reward from the current game-state plus a measure of the long-term future reward a controller expects to receive. Notice that, because the long term future reward depends on how the controller behaves in the future, the utility of a game-state depends on the controller.

To formalize the definition of utility, this section needs to introduce some additional notation taken from [RN02]. First, recall that percepts are a function of the game-state and that a controller is a function ϕ from percepts $\mathbf{x}$ to actions. The simulator is a function from the current game-state s and the controller's action choice $\phi(\mathbf{x})$ to a new game-state s'. More generally, a simulator can be thought of as a function T (called the transition model) that assigns probabilities to the possibility of ending up in a state s': $T(s, \phi(\mathbf{x}), s')$. The generalization might not be needed for the game simulator because it is typically deterministic. But, as seen from Section 6.4.2 in the previous chapter, the generalization is clearly needed for an approximate simulator.

Using the transition model, here is the formal recursive definition of the utility of a controller ϕ in a game-state s:

$$U^\phi(s) = R(s) + \gamma \sum_{s'} T(s, \phi(\mathbf{x}), s') \, U^\phi(s'), \qquad (7.1)$$

where $R(s)$ is the percept representing the current reward and γ is called the *discount factor*. The discount factor is a number between 0 and 1 where smaller numbers give more weight to short-term reward versus longer-term reward. Notice how the transition model is used to calculate the expected future utility over all the possible (as dictated by the possible actions) subsequent game-states s'.

If an NPC knows the utility of all states, it can behave optimally by picking actions that lead to states with the highest utility. Instead of a heuristic, it would be like having an oracle. A controller with access to an oracle does not need to search more than one step ahead. The next possible future game-state that the oracle says is best would necessarily be the optimal choice. Therefore, automatically learning a utility function would amount to learning to behave optimally.

7.4 Remembering

Normally, the idea of learning something implies some ability to generalize from past experience to new unseen cases. This is different from simply remembering what happened in the past and regurgitating it. Nevertheless, simple recall of past actions is a good place to start.

For example, consider the discrete tag game described at the start of the previous chapter. For now, assume that, except for the initial position of the tagged player, the game always starts in the same configuration and none of the other characters can move! If the tagged character has a path-planner like one described in the previous chapter, then when the tagged character plans a path to the nearest untagged character it ends up implicitly calculating the path cost. Suppose it also gets a reward for tagging a character, then the utility of the grid cell in which it started is set to the reward minus the path cost. The utility for each cell can be calculated in a similar manner. Notice, that by starting from the goal node and working outward, previous calculations can be re-used. That is, the utility of a path is always the utility of the current cell minus the cost to get there. This is,

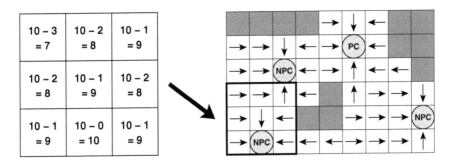

Figure 7.1. Induced vector field.

more or less, the intuition behind an algorithm called *dynamic programming* [SB98, RN02].

Once the utility of each cell has been calculated, the resulting values implicitly define a vector field. Figure 7.1 shows the vector field that results for one particular configuration. The inset on the left shows how the utility of each cell might be calculated. For example, the tagged character receives a reward of 10 whenever it gets to a cell containing an untagged character.[2] The utility of a cell is the reward available from the cell minus the least possible cost (using the Manhattan distance) of getting to the reward. The vector field is therefore induced by the direction of the adjacent cell with the highest utility. When there is a tie for the best utility among the adjacent cells, the figure arbitrarily shows just one of the optimal directions. At runtime, wherever the tagged character is placed, it can take the optimal route to the nearest untagged character by mindlessly following the vector field.

7.4.1 Function Approximation

Dropping the assumption that the game always starts in the same configuration leads to problems.[3] In the discrete tag game, with $m \times n$ grid

---

[2]Notice that the tagged character receives a reward for landing on the *same* cell as an untagged character. Previously the goal of the tagged character was stated as ending up in a cell *adjacent* to an untagged character. The only reason for the change is that the numbers in the figure are a bit more varied with the new rule.

[3]Note that this is also equivalent to letting the other characters move, since each subsequent board position will be equivalent to one of the initial configurations.

cells and k characters, there are (assuming at most one character per cell) a possible $\frac{(mn)!}{k!(mn-k)!}$ number of starting configurations. Storing a separate vector field for each of those configurations would obviously require a lot of memory and is therefore not practical.

Of course, by taking advantage of rotational symmetry, and other lossless compression techniques, memory usage could be minimized. A better solution, however, is to switch to a different representation. Instead of describing the current situation in terms of the game-state, use percepts. Percepts have been used throughout the book as a convenient and parsimonious representation for the game-state. As explained in Section 3.4 in Chapter 3, percepts hide unimportant details and emphasize crucial similarities between game-states. That is, they effectively act as a lossy way of compressing the game-state to leave only the information that is important to the AI algorithms.

Once a suitable collection of percepts has been defined an approximation to the table of vector fields can be learned. There are numerous possibilities for representing the approximation; popular choices are decision trees and neural networks. Depending on the chosen representation, various learning algorithms can be used to create a learned instance. The input to the learning would be a table of percept values, each line labeled with the corresponding average utility. Average utility is used because the percept values represent a set of possible game-states (i.e., a belief state) and so the calculated utility will vary depending on which (hidden) actual game-state the NPC is in. Of course, the table need never be explicitly computed; a planner is simply used to label examples, one at a time, from which the learner will learn. This is an example of a supervised learning *regression* problem. Unfortunately, the approach is unlikely to be successful because it ignores the fact that rewards in different states are not independent.

Instead of immediately considering alternatives, the next section drops the unrealistic assumption about movement taking place on a grid.

7.5 Reinforcement Learning

Reinforcement learning works by exploring the space of possible controllers to find ones that lead to high rewards. In particular, it looks for which actions, in which situations, lead to rewards. In the tag game, game level actions consist of two-dimensional direction vectors, which means that a controller is a mapping from percepts to $(R)^2$. That is a lot of possible different actions, so the space of possible controllers is enormous. It would therefore clearly be absurd to try and store the controller as a big table from percepts to actions. Without even having to go into details about how it might work, it should be clear that with so many possible actions, learning an approximation to the table would be hard. The problem is that, with so many actions, it would require too much data to explore the space well enough to spot any patterns that might occur. For example, the learner might notice that in some given situation it is a good idea to go in the direction $(0.6, 0.8)$. But without a lot more data it would not realize that in the same given situation any similar direction is probably also good.

It is therefore naive to expect to apply reinforcement learning directly to the problem of learning a controller in the tag game, or most other games. In the tag game, the actions used by the learned controller therefore need to be simplified and then fed into another subcontroller that will convert them into game actions. The next few subsections explore some possibilities for high-level actions that could be learned.

7.5.1 Compass Directions

Instead of a two-dimensional direction vector, a controller could learn in which of eight compass directions to move. The compass directions could then easily be somehow translated into a direction vector by a subcontroller.

Solely from a problem representation point of view, using compass directions makes the application of reinforcement learning feasible. However, the problem representation for the learner is still not nearly as simple as it could be. For example, suppose the tagged character has already learned to chase the nearest untagged character but that there is now an obstacle between it and its target. It will have to learn to go around the obstacle first, which may involve (in part) unlearning what it previously learned about heading directly toward its target. This will require a lot more data for it to figure out precisely under what circumstances it needs to take a detour before heading for its target. If a complicated maze was introduced into the tag game world, the situation becomes hopeless; the controller is never realistically going to learn to solve mazes and to reach the nearest character.

7.5.2 Waypoints

The waypoint graph introduced in Section 6.4 in the previous chapter can also be used for learning. In particular, the problem is to learn which waypoint to select as a goal. Once a waypoint is selected then control is handed over to a subcontroller that plans a path to the goal and follows the path. There would be some additional details to decide, such as how long the subcontroller should follow the path before it asks for a new goal; what it should do when it arrives at the goal; what it should do if it sees a nearby untagged character *en route*; etc. But assuming these details could be worked out the learning problem is now a lot easier. In particular, the path planning problem has been factored out of the equation.

The percepts that would be needed by the learner would be information about each of the waypoints, for example, whether there is an untagged character nearby, which direction the nearby character is heading, whether there is a large group of untagged characters nearby, etc. If the reward function is defined to give an extra reward to an NPC for tagging a character with whom it was angry, then there would also need to be percepts to provide information about whether there was a character with whom the NPC is angry near a waypoint.

To make the learning even easier the list of waypoints could be pre-filtered to just include a few promising ones. For example, the choice could just be between the waypoint with the nearest untagged character, or the waypoint with the nearest character with whom the tagged character is angry. Depending on how far each waypoint is, the directions the characters are traveling, and how the reward function is defined, a different waypoint could be the optimal one in different circumstances. The learning would figure out the trade-off on its own. Of course, if the problem is made simple enough, a different learning algorithm might be more appropriate.

The downside of simplifying the problem is that there will be less variety in the NPC's learned behavior. That is, if it has more action choices, then it has the potential to discover quirks about special situations that warrant a different response. By simplifying a problem you are biasing the learning to produce a certain kind of solution and there is less room for surprises. But if there are no surprises left at all, then you might have restricted the problem so tightly that it would be better off to just hand-code the one remaining solution that is left.

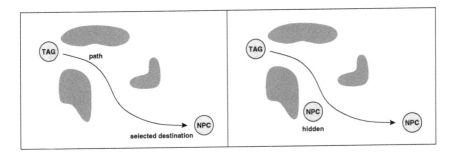

Figure 7.2. Two indistinguishable scenarios.

7.5.3 Transition Model

Another important consequence of simplifying the learning problem is that it introduces uncertainty. For example, Figure 7.2 shows two different scenarios in the tag game. In the scenario on the right-hand side, an NPC is hiding from the tagged character behind an obstacle. Assume that the percepts are correctly modeling the fact that the hidden NPC and the tagged character cannot see each other. Then from the learner's point of view both scenarios are indistinguishable.[4] In both cases the same waypoint will be selected and the tagged character will follow a path to that same waypoint. But in the scenario on the right, the tagged character may well stumble across the hidden NPC, who will be unable to see the tagged character coming. In the scenario on the left, no such good fortune will greet the tagged character and it is quite likely the NPC will see the tagged character coming and run away.

From the learner's point of view, the same action in two identical situations resulted in two different outcomes. The same ambiguity will also happen due to other sources of hidden information. Some of the information will be hidden deliberately; a lot more is simply not represented in the simplified model of the game-state represented in the percepts. The end result is that the learner sees the game world as noisy and full of uncertainty.

---

[4]This assumes there is no memory percept that records the last place a character was seen, as if there was, then the two situations in the figure are distinguishable. In such cases, an NPC could learn to explore areas near to where it last saw a character. But if in one case the hidden character had moved far away, but in another it had stayed near to where it was last seen, there would still be different outcomes. In general, partial observability always leads to uncertainty due to indistinguishable game-states.

x_0	x_1	x_2	x_3	...	a	x'_0	x'_1	x'_2	x_3	...	$T(\mathbf{x}, a, \mathbf{x'})$
f	N	b	E	...	b	f	S	c	E	...	0.02
f	N	b	W	...	g	b	S	f	W	...	0.04

Table 7.1. Two lines of an approximated transition model.

To make sense of its uncertain world, a learner can use its past experience to approximate the probabilities for the transition model that appears in Equation 7.1. That is, the learner uses a snapshot of itself so far as the controller and the associated NPC proceeds to interact with the game world. As the NPC moves around, performing actions in the game world, it can calculate the probability it will end up in some belief state $\mathbf{x'}$ given it performs an action a in belief state $\mathbf{x}$ as follows:

$$T(\mathbf{x}, a, \mathbf{x'}) = \frac{\text{number of times performing } a \text{ in } \mathbf{x} \text{ resulted in } \mathbf{x'}}{\text{number of times performed } a \text{ in } \mathbf{x}}.$$

For example, suppose in the approach described in Section 7.5.2 that there are (among many others) the following four percepts:

x_0 = The tagged character's current nearest waypoint,

x_1 = The tagged character's heading,

x_2 = The nearest untagged character's nearest waypoint,

x_3 = The nearest untagged character's heading.

Then probabilities in the approximate transition model table would look something like those in Table 7.1. Only two lines of the table are shown, and there is no significance meant to be attached to the values shown other than that they are of the right type. If the whole table was to be all written out explicitly it would have an enormous number of lines. But in principle, once the table has been determined, it can be used to calculate the expected utility of a belief state, and the action which leads to the belief state with the highest expected utility can be chosen. Therefore, once the transition model has been determined an NPC can use dynamic programming to calculate an optimal controller for that model.

But the NPC also does not have to wait until the transition model is fully acquired. At any point it can apply dynamic programming to the current transition model to get the best controller so far. This is called adaptive dynamic programming. It works because the transition model is a model of the environment and so is independent of the particular controller that has been learned so far. Unfortunately, for all but the simplest problems, it is often impractical to solve dynamic programming problems of the size that get generated in the adaptive dynamic programming approach.

To avoid solving large dynamic programming problems there are different methods of reinforcement learning. One particularly popular approach is called Q-learning. It has the advantage that, in a version called temporal difference Q-learning, the transition model probabilities are not explicitly required at all. The Q values represent the utility of performing an action a in game-state s, i.e., $Q(a, s)$. Q values can be learned with a relatively simple-looking update rule that is applied iteratively until the Q values converge:

$$Q(a, s) = Q(a, s) + \alpha(R(s) + \gamma \max_{a'} Q(a', s') - Q(a, s)),$$

where R is the reward, α is the learning rate, and γ is the discount factor.

7.5.4 Convergence

One reason reinforcement learning is popular is that if the world is fully observable it is guaranteed to converge to the optimal solution provided every action is performed an infinite number of times in every state. In practice, it often converges to a good solution after a long time of autonomously running millions of game simulations. Care also needs to be taken in practice that a wide variety of possible actions are tried in each state. Otherwise, if during learning the controller is too greedy to exploit what it has already learned, the learning can get stuck in a local minima. One way to ensure the learner properly explores the state space is to introduce some randomness by forcing the learning to not always pick the action that leads to the greatest expected utility. Instead, the learner only picks the best action with some probability. As the learner discovers more about its environment, the expected utility becomes more accurate and the learner can therefore explore less and exploit more. This can be done by gradually increasing the probability of picking the action with the greatest expected utility. Alternatively, the learner can be made to always be optimistic about the utility of actions it has not taken before in a given state.

When the game-state is only partially observable (through the percepts **x**) the theory underlying reinforcement learning is more complex. But in practice, it also often works provided the algorithm is run long enough and percepts are sufficiently well engineered to give the algorithm all the important information it needs. This is where games once again have an advantage over other AI application areas. In games, the percepts could (if necessary, and subject to concerns about realistic perception) be expanded to make the game-state fully observable. In other applications, the true underlying state of the world is often genuinely inaccessible and so optimism about percept engineering ultimately yielding success is less warranted.

In some nongame AI applications, running all the simulations required for reinforcement learning can take a long time and is risky. For example, if a robot makes a mistake and falls over a cliff it is a disaster. In games, simulation is cheap and the game world can easily be reset. In addition, if the renderer is decoupled from the rest of the game code, then running millions of simulations can be sped up by orders of magnitude.

You can read more about the topics of reinforcement learning, Q-learning, and learning in general in [Mit97, SB98, DHS00, HTF01, RN02].

7.5.5   Function Approximation

For any practical problem the state space is too large to explicitly store the Q-function (or transition model, if required) as a table. The table can therefore be represented by a function approximator like those described in Section 7.4.1. Unfortunately, the convergence guarantees also no longer apply if the Q-function is only approximated. But, as usual, it can often be made to work by changing percepts, adding percepts, or changing the problem representation.

There are articles in the games AI literature that suggest using a neural network as a function approximator. Neural networks can be used successfully, especially when (as in [Tes95]) there is an enormous amount of training data. But in general they are susceptible to problems because of the nature of the training samples. In particular, remember the learner is also the controller, so the training samples are not independent because they are generated by the learner itself. There is therefore potential for a harmful feedback loop: a learner generates experience that is used as input to a neural network that is used as the representation of the learner.

The neural network is, in effect, responsible for generating its own training data.

Other function approximators, like decision trees, do not suffer so much from the problem with feedback loops. The reason is that decision tree learning algorithms generalize training examples by interpolating, whereas neural networks can also extrapolate. Decision trees also have the desirable property that the output can be inspected to see if it looks somewhat reasonable. This is especially important if the algorithm is failing to converge as some important clues can be found by inspecting the decision trees being learned. In contrast, it is unlikely that staring at the weights of a neural network will reveal much useful information. For more about advanced research work on reinforcement learning, see [SJJ94, JSJ95, KLM96, Lit96, WS97, Per02].

Appendix A

Picking

The stochastic version of a controller described in Section 4.1.1 in Chapter 4 defines a probability distribution over possible actions. In this appendix, two common ways of picking a single action from a probability distribution are described: picking the most likely and picking randomly.

The descriptions assume some familiarity with basic mathematical probability. If you need a refresher course there are a huge number of references available on the underlying theory of mathematical probability. For example, a good standard textbook on the subject is [MMF04]. For a less formal presentation on some of the underlying intuitions, see [Isa96]. Also [RN02] and [KN03] include a lot of probability theory and references applicable to AI. Additional references, including to freely available resources on the Internet, are included on this book's companion web site.

There are, of course, other ways of measuring uncertainty besides probability, but probability is the optimal choice. It is optimal in the following sense: if you were playing a game that involved gambling and uncertainty, anyone using the laws of probability would do better (over the long haul) than a person using some other set of laws.

A.1   Picking the Most Likely

The simplest way to pick an action from a probability distribution is to pick the most likely one. For example, suppose there are five actions: $a_0, \ldots, a_4$ with probabilities as shown in Table A.1. Then the most likely action is a_1 because it has the largest associated probability.

a_i	a_0	a_1	a_2	a_3	a_4
$P(a_i|\mathbf{x})$	0.2	0.3125	0.25	0.0375	0.2

Table A.1. Example probability distribution.

If the probability distribution a controller is picking from is generated by some genuine real-world source of uncertainty, then picking the most likely action is a reasonable thing to do. However, in games, there are occasions when it can lead to unintended consequences. For example, suppose the probability distribution is fixed by the developer before the game ships as part of the character definition because the developer is presumably hoping that the probability distribution will introduce a bit of variety into the controller's decisions. However, the most likely action will always be the same one. There is no nondeterminism.

Even if the probability distribution is computed at runtime based on some inputs from the game world there can be problems. For example, in a simulated world it is common to find many examples of perfect symmetry. This can result in a probability distribution that assigns the same maximum probability to a set of actions, in which case, depending on the indexing order, the first action in the list will always be chosen. Two special cases of the problem are when all possible actions get the same probability, and when one single action is always given slightly more probability than any of the others. In the first case, picking the most likely is equivalent to picking the first action; and in the second, to always picking the same action.

A.2 Picking Randomly

Unless all the probabilities are the same, picking randomly according to a probability distribution does not mean that all actions have an equal chance of being selected. In particular, each action has the chance of being selected equal to its probability. For example, if a controller picked 50 actions using the probabilities in Table A.1, then you would expect it to pick action a_4 ten times. Of course, there is a small chance ($0.8^{50} \approx 0.0000143$) it would not pick a_4 at all, and an even smaller chance ($0.2^{50} \approx 0.11259 \times 10^{-34}$) it would pick a_4 every time.

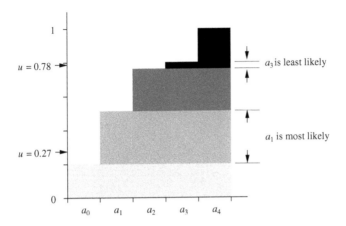

Figure A.1. Cumulative distribution.

Implementing a random pick according to a probability distribution is straightforward: use a random number generator to generate a (pseudo) random number u from the uniform distribution between 0 and 1. Then, add up the probabilities of each action one at a time until they equal or exceed u. The action whose probability caused the running total to equal or exceed u is the choice. For example, using the probability distribution in Table A.1, if the random number generator picks $u = 0.27$, then action a_1 (the most likely) is chosen. Figure A.1 shows the cumulative distribution and how it is used to pick an action given the value of u.

Notice that if the random number generator had picked $u = 0.78$, say, then the least likely action a_3 would have been picked. Depending on the game, having the (even remote) possibility of picking such low-probability actions might be undesirable. If so, it is straightforward to filter out the low-probability events, renormalize, and then pick according to the new distribution.

Be careful to have only one instance of a random number generator in your game and seed it just once at the start. That way, for a given seed, you will always get the same sequence of random numbers. If the inputs are kept the same, you will therefore get the same number of calls to the single random number generator, which will, in turn, produce the same simulation every time. This will help you track down the source of errors when you are debugging because the bug will be easily reproducible.

Obviously if the input changes, such as when a player is playing the game, the random sequence will quickly diverge. That is a good thing as, once the game ships, players do not want to see the same simulation every time. To be extra careful, the shipped version of the game can alternate between different initial seeds.

Appendix B

Programming

C++ code snippets are used throughout this book to make concepts clearer and more concrete. To understand the C++ code you obviously need to have some degree of familiarity with programming in an object-oriented programming language like C++. As software engineering practices become more refined, C++ is displacing C as the most popular language for game development. All the major game development platforms have a choice of C++ compilers available and provided the programmer is careful to avoid some common pitfalls (see [Ise04]), it is at least as efficient as C.

Like C++, Java is another popular object-oriented programming language. For games that appear within web pages and on mobile devices it might make a good choice, but at the time of writing it is not well supported on the major console platforms. Among AI researchers in academia, LISP has traditionally been widely used and it has also enjoyed some popularity among game developers. The company Naughty Dog used Allegro CL to create GOOL (Game Object-Oriented Language) for use in programming their successful Crash Bandicoot series. Since being acquired by Sony, the same team plans to use LISP even more extensively in future titles. Nevertheless, LISP is not widely known in the game development community, so C++ remains the most reasonable choice for code given in this book. It should be straightforward for an experienced programmer to translate the code (or at least the underlying ideas) to other programming languages.

Games development used to be notorious for bad software engineering practices. Some of this was justified by the fact that games were often written as one-off, throw-away, applications. Companies also like to

rewrite their games from release to release to give them a fresh feel. But
so many games are now building on previous codebases, or using game
engines across projects, that good software engineering is becoming a ne-
cessity. Even within a single project, games are becoming so complex that
sloppy coding practices can cause development times to grow needlessly.
Numerous good references and pointers to online resources about software
engineering are therefore available on this book's companion web site.

Here are a few miscellaneous notes about the code in this book:

- the code has been written to make it as easy to understand as possible, and it is often therefore not particularly efficient. In particular,
  there is little or no caching of previous results as that would add
  complexity to the code. For example, in the tgGameState class introduced in Chapter 2 it would make sense to have a private class
  variable characterIndices to store the list of indices of those objects
  that are characters. This would make it faster to iterate through the
  characters and return a pointer to a requested character. As the code
  stands, many simple operations would require searching through the
  whole list of game objects to find the desired one(s). Another place
  where caching is important is in the calculation of percepts, but care
  has to be taken to correctly purge and manage the caches as the
  myIndex variable changes.

- class methods in this book often use the "get" prefix for accessors
  to class member variables and "calc" methods that actually need to
  do some work. However, the convention is only followed laxly as,
  depending on the underlying implementation, some methods could
  be defined either way around.

- the code given in this book makes limited use of the Standard Tem-
  plate Library (STL) (see www.sgi.com/tech/stl) as it is convenient
  and greatly simplifies some of the code. However, to use STL in
  your own games you might need to write your own custom memory
  allocation routines (see [Ise02]).

- AI code often depends on a number of geometric calculations. These
  calculations resolve various geometric relationships between entities
  in the game world. A simple example is determining the distance between an NPC and its nearest enemy. A more complex example is

determining whether an NPC can be seen from its current location. Some kind of linear algebra package is required to perform the relevant calculations. The code in this book assumes the existence of a class tgVec for performing linear algebra calculations. Operator overloading is *not* used as it can easily lead to confusing code. This book's companion web site has some links to some freely available linear algebra packages that could be used in games. For the simple linear algebra used in most games it is also not hard to write your own package from scratch.

- aside from methods for geometric calculations, there are some other methods that are referenced but never defined. In such cases the semantics of the method should hopefully be obvious from the name.

- the code given in this book does not contain much error checking. Error checking is important in debug releases of code and there are many books on software engineering that cover the topic.

- the code in this book is not console-compliant. For example, the code creates objects whenever it needs to, which can lead to memory fragmentation. To avoid this, consoles typically use a pool or a stack memory manager that preallocates space when the game first starts up.

- all the objects in the tag game are declared in the tagGame namespace. The "tg" prefix is therefore not strictly necessary, but serves to avoid ending up with variable names that clash with reserved words (similarly for the "dtg" prefix used in the discrete tag game).

- the code in this book might not be formatted to your taste. For example, you might prefer to write your if-statements with the curly bracket on the same line, or put the **const** designator before the type, or use sophisticated naming schemes for variables, etc. There is not much to write about such issues, except that most of the choices in this book have some rationale behind them, but ultimately it comes down to a matter of personal taste.

Bibliography

[AC87]   Philip E. Agre and David Chapman. Pengi: A Theory of
            Activity. In *Proceedings of AAAI 87*, 1987.

[aiS00]   aiSee. Graph Visualization. Available from World Wide
            Web (www.aisee.com), 2000.

[AL98]   Natasha Alechina and Brian Logan. State space Search with
            Prioritised Soft Constraints. In *Proceedings of the ECAI
            98 Workshop: Decision Theory meets Artificial Intelligence*,
            1998.

[Ale02]   Thor Alexander. GoCap: Game Observation Capture. In
            Steve Rabin, editor, *AI Game Programming Wisdom*. Charles
            River Media, Hingham, MA, 2002.

[BDI+02]   Bruce Blumberg, Marc Downie, Yuri Ivanov, Matt Berlin,
            Michael Patrick Johnson, and Bill Tomlinson. Integrated
            Learning for Interactive Synthetic Characters. In *Proceed-
            ings of ACM SIGGRAPH 2002*, Computer Graphics Proceed-
            ings, Annual Conference Series, 2002.

[Ber04]   Curt Bererton. State Estimation for Game AI Using Particle
            Filters. In *AAAI Workshop on Challenges in Game AI*, 2004.

[BM98]   C.L. Blake and C.J. Merz. UCI Repository of Machine
            Learning Databases. Available from World Wide Web
            (www.ics.uci.edu/~mlearn/MLRepository.html), 1998.

[Bou01]   David M. Bourg. *Physics for Game Developers*. O'Reilly &
            Associates, Sebastopol, CA, 2001.

[Bra84]   Valentino Braitenberg. *Vehicles: Experiments in Synthetic Psychology*. MIT Press, Cambridge, MA, 1984.

[Bro90]   Rodney A. Brooks. Elephants Don't Play Chess. *Robotics and Autonomous Systems*, 6(1&2), 1990.

[Cha91]   David Chapman. *Vision, Instruction, and Action*. MIT Press, Cambridge, MA, 1991.

[Cha03]   Alex J. Champandard. *AI Game Development*. New Riders, Indianapolis, IN, 2003.

[DB04]   Richard C. Dorf and Robert H. Bishop. *Modern Control Systems*. Prentice Hall, Upper Saddle River, NJ, tenth edition, 2004.

[DEdGD04]   Jonathan Dinerstein, Parris K Egbert, Hugo de Garis, and Nelson Dinerstein. Fast and Learnable Behavioral and Cognitive Modeling for Virtual Character Animation. *Computer Animation and Virtual Worlds*, 15(2), 2004.

[DeL00]   Mark DeLoura, editor. *Game Programming Gems*. Charles River Media, Hingham, MA, 2000.

[DeL01]   Mark DeLoura, editor. *Game Programming Gems 2*. Charles River Media, Hingham, MA, 2001.

[DHS00]   Richard O. Duda, Peter E. Hart, and David G. Stork. *Pattern Classification*. Wiley, New York, NY, 2000.

[Doy02]   Patrick Doyle. Believability through Context: Using Knowledge in the World to Create Intelligent Characters. In *Proceedings of the International Joint Conference on Autonomous Agents and Multi-Agent Systems (AAMAS 2002)*, 2002.

[Etz93]   Oren Etzioni. Intelligence without Robots (A Reply to Brooks). *AI Magazine*, 14(4), 1993.

[Fal95]   Petros Faloutsos. Physics-based animation and control of flexible characters. Master's thesis, University of Toronto, 1995.

[Fun99]   John D. Funge. *AI for Animation and Games: A Cognitive Modeling Approach*. A K Peters, Wellesley, MA, 1999.

[FvDFH95]   James D. Foley, Andries van Dam, Steven K. Feiner, and John F. Hughes. *Computer Graphics: Principles and Practice in C*. Addison-Wesley, Reading, MA, second edition, 1995.

[FvdPT01]   Petros Faloutsos, Michiel van de Panne, and Demetri Terzopoulos. Composable Controllers for Physics-Based Character Animation. In *Proceedings of ACM SIGGRAPH 2001*, Computer Graphics Proceedings, Annual Conference Series, 2001.

[Gib87]   James J. Gibson. *The Ecological Approach to Visual Perception*. Lawrence Erlbaum Associates, Mahwah, NJ, 1987.

[GT95]   Radek Grzeszczuk and Demetri Terzopoulos. Automated Learning of Muscle-Actuated Locomotion Through Control Abstraction. In *Proceedings of SIGGRAPH 95*, Computer Graphics Proceedings, Annual Conference Series, 1995.

[HF03]   Ryan Houlette and Dan Fu. The Ultimate Guide to FSMs in Games. In Steve Rabin, editor, *AI Game Programming Wisdom 2*. Charles River Media, Hingham, MA, 2003.

[HP97]   Jessica K. Hodgins and Nancy S. Pollard. Adapting Simulated Behaviors for New Characters. In *Proceedings of SIGGRAPH 97*, Computer Graphics Proceedings, Annual Conference Series, 1997.

[HTF01]   Trevor Hastie, Robert Tibshirani, and Jerome Friedman. *The Elements of Statistical Learning*. Springer-Verlag, New York, NY, 2001.

[IB02]   Damian Isla and Bruce Blumberg. Object Persistence for Synthetic Creatures. In *Proceedings of the International Joint Conference on Autonomous Agents and Multiagent Systems (AAMAS)*, 2002.

[Isa96]   Richard Isaac. *The Pleasures of Probability*. Springer-Verlag, New York, NY, 1996.

[Ise02]   Pete Isensee. Custom STL Allocators. In Dante Treglia and Mark DeLoura, editors, *Game Programming Gems 3*. Charles River Media, Hingham, MA, 2002.

[Ise04]   Pete Isensee. Common C++ Performance Mistakes in Games. In *Game Developer's Conference Proceedings*, 2004.

[JSJ95]   Tommi Jaakkola, Satinder P. Singh, and Michael I. Jordan. Reinforcement Learning Algorithms for Partially Observable Markov Problems. In *Advances in Neural Information Processing Systems 7, Proceedings of the 1994 Conference*, 1995.

[KGP02]   Lucas Kovar, Michael Gleicher, and Frédéric Pighin. Motion Graphs. *ACM Transactions on Graphics*, 21(3), 2002.

[Kin00]   Melianthe Kines. Planning and Directing Motion Capture for Games. *Gamasutra*, 2000.

[Kir04]   Andrew Kirmse, editor. *Game Programming Gems 4*. Charles River Media, Hingham, MA, 2004.

[KL00]   James Kuffner and Steven M. LaValle. RRT-Connect: An Efficient Approach to Single-Query Path Planning. In *Proceedings of the IEEE International Conference on Robotics and Automation (ICRA 2000)*, 2000.

[KLM96]   Leslie Pack Kaelbling, Michael L. Littman, and Andrew P. Moore. Reinforcement Learning: A Survey. *Journal of Artificial Intelligence Research*, 4, 1996.

[KN03]   Kevin B. Korb and Ann E. Nicholson. *Bayesian Artificial Intelligence*. CRC Press, Boca Raton, FL, 2003.

[KS96]   Henry Kautz and Bart Selman. Pushing the Envelope: Planning, Propositional Logic, and Stochastic Search. In *Proceedings of the Thirteenth National Conference on Artificial Intelligence*, 1996.

[KS03]   Henry Kautz and Bart Selman. Ten Challenges Redux: Recent Progress in Propositional Reasoning and Search. In *Proceedings of the Ninth International Conference on Principles and Practice of Constraint Programming (CP 2003)*, 2003.

[LCR03]   Greg Lawrence, Noah Cowan, and Stuart Russell. Efficient Gradient Estimation for Motor Control Learning. In *Proceedings of the Nineteenth Conference on Uncertainty in Artificial Intelligence*, 2003.

[LDG03]   Seth Luisi, Glenn Van Datta, and Bob Gutmann. SOCOM: Bringing a Console Game Online. In *Game Developer's Conference Proceedings*, 2003.

[Len95]   Douglas B. Lenat. CYC: A Large-Scale Investment in Knowledge Infrastructure. *Communications of the ACM*, 38(11), 1995.

[Leo03]   Tom Leonard. Building an ai Sensory System: Examining the Design of Thief: The Dark Project. In *Game Developer's Conference Proceedings*, 2003.

[Lin98]   Fangzhen Lin. Applications of the Situation Calculus to Formalizing Control and Strategic Information: The Prolog Cut Operator. *Artificial Intelligence*, 103(1&2), 1998.

[Lit96]   Michael Lederman Littman. *Algorithms for Sequential Decision Making*. PhD thesis, Brown University, 1996.

[LNR87]   John E. Laird, Allan Newell, and Paul S. Rosenbloom. SOAR: An Architecture of General Intelligence. *Artificial Intelligence*, 33(3), 1987.

[LvdPF00]   Joseph Laszlo, Michiel van de Panne, and Eugene L. Fiume. Interactive Control for Physically-Based Animation. In *Proceedings of ACM SIGGRAPH 2000*, Computer Graphics Proceedings, Annual Conference Series, 2000.

[Man03]   John Manslow. Using Reinforcement Learning to Solve AI Control Problems. In Steve Rabin, editor, *AI Game Programming Wisdom 2*. Charles River Media, Hingham, MA, 2003.

[Mar01]   Richard Marks. Using Video Input for Games. In *Game Developer's Conference Proceedings*, 2001.

[Mit97]   Tom M. Mitchell. *Machine Learning*. McGraw-Hill, New York, NY, 1997.

[MMF04]   Irwin Miller, Marylees Miller, and John E. Freund. *John E. Freund's Mathematical Statistics with Applications*. Prentice Hall, Upper Saddle River, NJ, seventh edition, 2004.

[MNPW98]   Nicola Muscettola, P. Pandurang Nayak, Barney Pell, and Brian C. Williams. Remote Agent: To Boldly Go Where No AI System Has Gone Before. *Artificial Intelligence*, 103(1&2), 1998.

[MS99]   Christopher D. Manning and Hinrich Schütze. *Foundations of Statistical Natural Language Processing*. MIT Press, Cambridge, MA, 1999.

[Osb03]   Martin J. Osborne. *An Introduction to Game Theory*. Oxford University Press, New York, NY, 2003.

[Pea84]   Judea Pearl. *Heuristics: Intelligent Search Strategies for Computer Problem Solving*. Addison-Wesley, Reading, MA, 1984.

[Per02]   Theodore J. Perkins. Reinforcement Learning for POMDPs Based on Action Values and Stochastic Optimization. In *Proceedings of the Eighteenth National Conference on Artificial Intelligence*, 2002.

[Rab00]   Steve Rabin. A* Aesthetic Optimizations. In Mark De-Loura, editor, *Game Programming Gems*. Charles River Media, Hingham, MA, 2000.

[Rab02]   Steve Rabin, editor. *AI Game Programming Wisdom*. Charles River Media, Hingham, MA, 2002.

[Rab03a]   Steve Rabin, editor. *AI Game Programming Wisdom 2*. Charles River Media, Hingham, MA, 2003.

[Rab03b]   Steve Rabin. Game AI Articles and Research. Available
            from World Wide Web (www.aiwisdom.com), 2003.

[Rei01]   Raymond Reiter. *Knowledge in Action: Logical Foundations
            for Specifying and Implementing Dynamical Systems.* MIT
            Press, Cambridge, MA, 2001.

[Rey87]   Craig W. Reynolds. Flocks, Herds, and Schools: A Dis-
            tributed Behavioral Model. In *Computer Graphics (Proceed-
            ings of SIGGRAPH 87)*, Computer Graphics Proceedings,
            Annual Conference Series, 1987.

[Rey99]   Craig Reynolds. Steering Behaviors for Autonomous Char-
            acters. In *Game Developer's Conference Proceedings*, 1999.

[RG03]   Christopher Reed and Benjamin Geisler. Jumping, Climbing,
            and Tactical reasoning: How to Get More Out of a Naviga-
            tion System. In Steve Rabin, editor, *AI Game Programming
            Wisdom 2*. Charles River Media, Hingham, MA, 2003.

[RN02]   Stuart Russell and Peter Norvig. *Artificial Intelligence: A
            Modern Approach.* Prentice Hall, Upper Saddle River, NJ,
            second edition, 2002.

[Sam02]   Miro Samek. *Practical Statecharts in C/C++*. CMP Books,
            Gilroy, CA, 2002.

[SB98]   Richard S. Sutton and Andrew G. Barto. *Reinforcement
            Learning: An Introduction.* MIT Press, Cambridge, MA,
            1998.

[Shi02]   Peter Shirley. *Fundamentals of Computer Graphics*. A K Pe-
            ters, Wellesley, MA, 2002.

[SJJ94]   Satinder P. Singh, Tommi Jaakkola, and Michael I. Jor-
            dan. Learning without State-Estimation in Partially Ob-
            servable Markovian Decision Processes. In *Proceedings of
            the Eleventh International Conference on Machine Learning*,
            1994.

[SP96]   Aaron Sloman and Riccardo Poli. SIM AGENT: A Toolkit
            for Exploring Agent Designs. In Mike Wooldridge, Joerg
            Mueller, and Milind Tambe, editors, *Intelligent Agents Vol II
            (ATAL-95)*. Springer-Verlag, New York, NY, 1996.

[TD02]   Dante Treglia and Mark DeLoura, editors. *Game Program-
            ming Gems 3*. Charles River Media, Hingham, MA, 2002.

[Tes95]   Gerald Tesauro. Temporal Difference Learning and TD-
            Gammon. *Communications of the ACM*, 38(3), 1995.

[TR97]   Demetri Terzopoulos and Tamer Rabie. Animat Vision: Ac-
            tive Vision in Artificial Animals. *Videre: Journal of Com-
            puter Vision Research*, 1(1), 1997.

[vdB03]   Gino van den Bergen. *Collision Detection in Interactive 3D
            Environments*. Morgan Kaufmann, San Francisco, CA, 2003.

[vdS02]   William van der Sterren. Tactical Path-Finding with A*. In
            Dante Treglia and Mark DeLoura, editors, *Game Program-
            ming Gems 3*. Charles River Media, Hingham, MA, 2002.

[vW01]   Jean Paul van Waveren. The quake III arena bot. Master's
            thesis, Delft University of Technology, 2001.

[WB01]   Andrew Witkin and David Baraff. Physically based model-
            ing. SIGGRAPH 2001 Course Notes, 2001.

[WF99]   Ian H. Witten and Eibe Frank. *Data Mining: Practical Ma-
            chine Learning Tools and Techniques with Java Implementa-
            tions*. Morgan Kaufmann, San Francisco, CA, 1999.

[WM03]   Ian Wright and James Marshall. The Execution Kernel of
            RC++: RETE*, a Faster RETE with TREAT as a Special
            Case. *International Journal of Intelligent Games and Simu-
            lation*, 2(1), 2003.

[Wol02]   Stephen Wolfram. *A New Kind of Science*. Wolfram Media,
            Champaign, IL, 2002.

[Wri97]   Ian Wright. Emotional agents. Master's thesis, University of Birmingham, 1997.

[WS97]   Marco Wiering and Jüurgen Schmidhuber.   HQ-Learning. *Adaptive Behavior*, 6(2), 1997.

[WW04]   Will Wright and Mike Winter. Stupid Fun Club. Available from World Wide Web (www.stupidfunclub.com), 2004.

Index